S. Nicoletti

Gold Conspiracy

The worst financial system in the world - how the bankers get rich and all

others get poor

S. Nicoletti

Gold Conspiracy
The worst financial system in the world - how the bankers get rich and all others get poor

ISBN/EAN: 9783337119706

Printed in Europe, USA, Canada, Australia, Japan

Cover: Foto ©Suzi / pixelio.de

More available books at **www.hansebooks.com**

A GOLD CONSPIRACY

OR

The Worst Financial System in the World,

HOW THE BANKERS GET RICH

AND

ALL OTHERS GET POOR,

A radical change needed.

———•◆•———

BY

CAPT. S. NICOLETTI

OF

LOS ANGELES, CAL.

———

Fully Illustrated.

———

Giving the dates of all the most important Laws passed by Congress, pertaining to the money question, and Other Illustrations.

PUBLISHED BY

The Progressive American Publishing Company of New York.
1896.

CONTENTS.

PREFACE TO THE SECOND EDITION.

Since the publication of this book I have received numerous letters of commendation from all classes of people, among them a great many prominent citizens, besides the sale has proved so satisfactory that not a single copy is left of the first edition. In order to comply with the general demand for this book, it affords me pleasure to issue a second and more complete edition in which any errors in the first edition have been corrected. What I predicted in my public addresses three years ago, came to pass as I prophesied. The friends of true *financial Reform* will undoubedly aid me in my efforts to down the evils now existing, but it is not sufficient that they send me only words of approval. The works of propaganda must be pushed vigorously, fearlessly, and without relenting. This is the true key to *Success.* The war-cry should be: " *Equal Rights for All, Special Privileges to None.*" " *Equality before the Law.*"

Most Sincerely Yours,
STEPHEN NICOLETTI.

WASHINGTON, D. C., 1896.

From among the thousands of letters that I have received, I select a few at random, not having space to insert here all the kind words of approval addressed to me.

614 NORTH BROAD STREET, PHILADELPHIA.

OFFICE OF GENERAL ASSEMBLY

Order of Knights of Labor

Philadelphia, Pa., March 21, 1895.

Captain S. Nicoletti,
192 Worth St.,
New York City, N.Y.

Dear Sir and Brother:--Replying to yours of the 2, inst., I am pleased to say that after examining your book "A Gold Conspiracy," I am fully convinced that it should be read by the working people of this entire nation. It is full of pointed matter, striking illustrations and unimpeachable facts and you deserve the congratulations of all reformers for its compilation and publication. I have not now in my possession a copy of the bank circular to which you refer.

Wishing you the greatest possible measure of success and happiness, I am,

Fraternally yours,

DO YOU READ?

Are you posted on the money question? If not, you will derive in this book the study of a lifetime on the subject, and it will put you in a position where you can give points to the sound (?), fake Financier of Ohio. It is an important question, which has agitated the whole world since its beginning, and is put so plain that no one can fail to understand and know it thoroughly.

TESTIMONIALS.

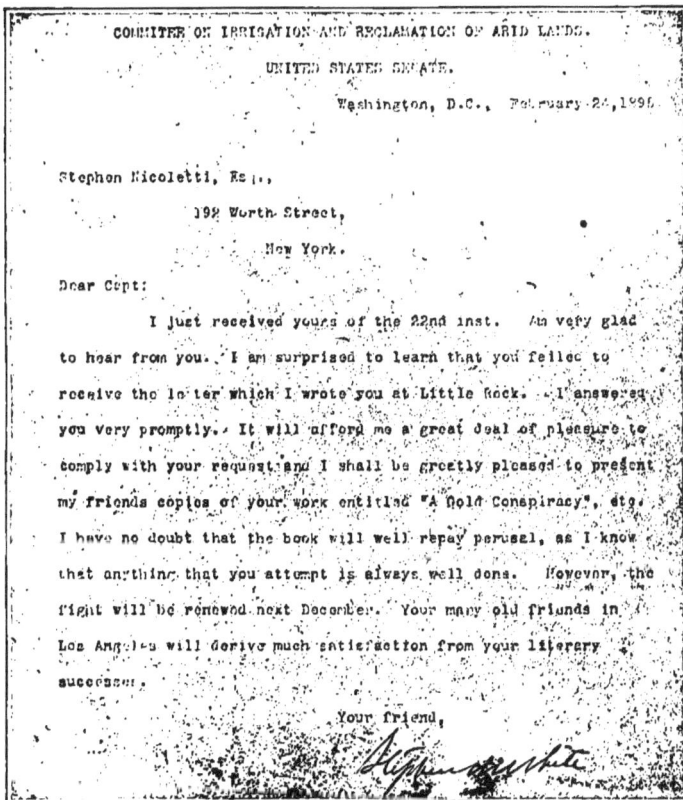

COMMITTEE ON IRRIGATION AND RECLAMATION OF ARID LANDS.

UNITED STATES SENATE.

Washington, D.C., February 24, 1896.

Stephen Nicoletti, Esq.,

    192 Worth Street,

        New York.

Dear Sir:

    I just received yours of the 22nd inst. Am very glad to hear from you. I am surprised to learn that you failed to receive the letter which I wrote you at Little Rock. I answered you very promptly. It will afford me a great deal of pleasure to comply with your request and I shall be greatly pleased to present my friends copies of your work entitled "A Gold Conspiracy", etc. I have no doubt that the book will well repay perusal, as I know that anything that you attempt is always well done. However, the fight will be renewed next December. Your many old friends in Los Angeles will derive much satisfaction from your literary success.

            Your friend,

U. S. Senator from Cal.
Chairman of Democratic National Convention.

GENERAL OFFICES

American Railway Union,

EUGENE V. DEBS, President.
GEORGE W. HOWARD, Vice-Pres.
SYLVESTER KEIHER, Secretary.

March 7, 1895.

Capt. S. Nicoletti,

192 North Street, New York City.

My dear Sir:-

Your kind favor of the 2nd instant to Mr. Debs is before me as also are the four copies of your work, "A Gold Conspiracy." Mr. Debs is in North Dakota and will likely spend some time on the Pacific coast before his return. I can assure you he is a busy man and if he does not comply with each request you make it will be because of lack of opportunity. I have reviewed your book briefly with much satisfaction. It is calculated to make those who read it think. That is supplying the greatest demand of the reform movement to-day. If working men could be induced to think their emancipation would be assured.

I will take pleasure in bringing your letter and books to the personal notice of Mr. Debs when he returns. Thank you very much for your kindness.

Yours very truly,

[signature] Benedict,
Private Secretary.

It is pronounced by all intelligent people and best thinkers to be the ablest product on the financial question of any modern literary effort.

INTRODUCTION.

Conscience, humanity and experience are the causes for the writing of this book, to call the attention of the public to the extravagance and corruption existing for many years in our general government, and how the "Favored Few" have accumulated millions, while the masses of producers have been pauperized by special laws and class legislation, passed one at a time by the money power tools at our capital (Washington, D. C.) which the writer will quote and any one can satisfy himself by investigating them and verify the assertion and truth in these matters.

For this condition of affairs we are all to blame; while we have been neglecting our duties as citizens, the shrewd Bankers have held high carnival and with their potent influence of money for "corrupt" purposes they have established the gold standard against the wish of the people, who now commence to see it, and the writer hopes that the importance of this book will be understood by the intelligent readers, for whom I have the highest respect, and I know they have not the time to read long books, for which reason I make this a small one (Brevity) as their time is valuable, touching lightly upon the various and most important laws on the subject, and as I attack the monster of the land, the money power (or the interest), the most important question that has agitated the world, and it domains, this free land. It is so deeply radicated that it seems impossible to some people to eradicate it without a war! and to cure such wrongs that keep the masses of the people slaves to King Gold, whom no one could get a square meal out of if he had all the gold that the world possesses.

He must go and till the land, that with Labor produces the necessaries of life, and it is the basis of all resources and values; gold and silver, etc. comes from the land, but no land can ever come from gold. You can easily procure gold by having land if you choose to pay the Shylock-owners interest on it. If it was not for the vicious laws that have been passed, gold would not be held so high as money, or medium of exchange. Silver would have held its place as a money metal, which it has been for a long time past.

Now I honestly believe in a currency or medium of exchange based on the brain, blood, muscles and land, or the wealth of the whole people of this great land.

A paper money, Greenbacks. a full legal tender for all debts, public or private, are issued by the Government direct to the people, according to the necessity and demand. Now, a money with the above backing to it is better than gold and silver, (for it includes both of said metals) for paper money has flourished in the past, and has twice saved this great Nation, to wit, in 1812 and 1861, and ancient history tells us that when past nations have adopted gold as their only money or medium of exchange, (that we must have to facilitate commerce) the Shylock owners of it have become so oppressive and tyrannical, that the people have revolted and destroyed them, and civilization with them. Greece, Persia, Egypt and Rome are examples.

Now, Venice the longest republic that the world ever saw, and perhaps never to be equaled, to wit, over six hundred years, from 1100 to 1797, had a paper money that was taken at a premium by all the civilized world, and the Republic flourished and Venice was the Queen of the Sea and the center of commerce until Napoleon entered her gates and took down that paper money and replaced it with coward gold money, that has reduced her from the Queen of the Sea and the center of commerce, to a mere museum for tourists to visit, Those are Examples that our congressmen can find out in our public libraries.

It will not be very long before England, the coarsest Isle of the world, with her *octopus* gold lords, who suck the blood of all who labor to pay them the interest on it, will have her turn of oblivion as a Government, that is trying, and has succeeded in dictating our Financial System, and for which she got the benefit and best of it.

Very respectfully yours,

New York, Feb. 1895.   Capt. S. NICOLETTI.

A GOLD CONSPIRACY.

The Money or Finance question has been written on before by many different writers and financiers, and they have so complicated the question about grains and fineness, that it is less understood by the common people than any other question, and the shrewd and "cunning" bankers have been always planning ahead how to mislead the people from knowing how things are being conducted by them in such an important and vital question; and they have, and still use, the "corrupt" Press to their advantage, and have succeeded in their work, so that they now get the crops every time, rain or shine, or get the farms, which is the case seventy times out of every one hundred. They have had laws passed by their tools in both branches of Congress and by the President also, for the last twenty-five or thirty years, so that they can, if they desire, throw the country into a financial panic at the tick of a telegram or by secret circulars, as they have done for the last two years, and in the past, to force legislation in their favor, and they still persist with their schemes until they have accomplished their work, which is to perpetuate their prey of usury on the American people, to wit: to continue and keep on issuing more Government bonds ; that is their intent, and they have already secured $100,000,000 new ones last year with promise of more which means more interest for them and more burdens for the people. They have gone too far and must be stopped, as millions of people have been killed and starved to carry out their schemes, which are fearlessly shown in this book, and it is the duty of every true, good American citizen to intelligently act and use his influence towards others for the stopping of the present condition of affairs that have been for the benefit of bankers, as the present and other administrations have done.

Now let us see what Money is. Money is a representative of labor and property used as medium of exchange, or a circulating medium. If it is a circulating medium is it right to lock it up? *No,* because it is necessary for the transaction of business, and it is impossible to carry property and performed labor in our pockets from place to place.

The writer claims that money is to trades and commerce a blood running through their channel and veins, like the circulation of blood through the veins and channels of a person. Now if the blood of the said person does not circulate freely as the regular circulation demands it, or if it becomes scarce, the said person is sure to become sick and he quickly goes to a doctor to get cured from the disease and improve his blood system.

And if money does not circulate freely in the veins and channels of commerce, or if it becomes scarce (the little that is in the hands of the few will increase in value if locked up) commerce and business will become sick and at a standstill, and this is the kind of sickness that our country is suffering from to-day and has been suffering from for many years, for not having a pure and perfect Financial system.

The doctors to cure this kind of sickness are at Washington, D. C., Congress, Senate,and the President, and they are sent there by the people to do the best thing that is necessary for the betterment of the whole people of our country, and not for the benefit of the few Gold Bugs, and the Gold Lords of England.

The said doctors ought to care for and cure the country that pays them for it, and they have the prescriptions and the medicine there, too, if they only use it, put there by better doctors than they, to wit: the framers of our Constitution of the United States, which says in Section VIII (8) Article V (5) "Congress has power to coin money and fix the value thereof," and Senator Voorhees of Indiana, Chairman of the Senate Finance Committee says in his speech for the repeal of the Sherman Silver purchasing act: that Congress had power to coin money and fix the value thereof, and also said that Congress was creator of money and fixed the value of it, and the Supreme Court of the United States affirmed said power in the decision of the case of August D. Jullard *vs.* Thomas S. Greenman, decided March 3, 1884.

The court held that under the Constitution Congress has power, if it deems it expedient, to issue legal tender notes to any amount, either in time of peace or war. For this decision. see United States Report, No. 110, Page 421.

In rendering this decision, the court reversed two prior decisions, in which the court stood divided; but in this case delivered the decision written by Justice Gray, which was concurred in by eight Judges, only Justice Field dissenting.

This decision has been upheld by the court ever since, also in many States, and it stands. Where can a plainer and more conclusive language than the one which the court used be found? The present administration should understand this and instead of issuing bonds, should issue legal tender notes when there is need to meet the expenses of the Government. Why don't they do so? Legal tender notes are a non-interest bearing debt, and bonds are an interest bearing debt that enriches the bankers and pauperizes the people, because the bankers want the interest, and the administration gives it.

Coxey, Kelly, and other's armies, demanded the starting of work from those deaf but well-fed doctors at our employ ; while millions of producers are suffering with their families, the bankers' tools roll in luxury at the people's expense at Washington, and instead of doing their duty to the people, they fillibuster and halloo to stop legislating for the people and their country, and sometimes they go and have good times with some poor innocent girl, even if they are married, and then they teach lies about morality, as we all have read of the Pollard-Breckenridge scandal, and who knows how many more are doing the same thing and it is kept secret.

We can settle this very important question in an intelligent way—that is by the discharging of those doctors from our service at Election Day, by electing doctors that will work and work for the people, honest men and not lawyers "corrupt" millionaires, and politicians that do not know what hard work is ; by so doing we will save our country and our institutions and show to the world that our civilization is founded and bound to reign above all civilizations that the world has ever seen, and it is the duty of every American citizen, as I said before, to put his shoulder to the wheel and push for the betterment of the masses and quit pushing for the bankers that are hallooing for more, more bonds. When we elect such doctors as Washington, Jefferson, Jackson or Lincoln. no money power can use them and none like them have been elected to the presidential chair for the last thirty years.

THE HISTORY OF PAPER MONEY AND WHAT IT HAS ACCOMPLISHED
IN THE PAST FOR THE GOOD OF THIS GREAT COUNTRY.

FIRST PAPER MONEY IN THE UNITED STATES.

The first paper money, or treasury notes, issued under authority of Congress, was during the war against England in 1812. The first treasury notes were issued on June 20th, 1812, and from said date to February 24th, 1815, sixty million and five hundred thousand dollars were issued, bearing interest at five and two-fifths per cent. per annum, and they were a full legal tender for all dues to the government, for taxes and for other payments. Another Act was passed on the 24th of February, 1815, for the additional issue of twenty-five millions, and all the notes of a denomination of one hundred dollars and upwards bore interest at five and two-fifths per cent. per annum, and were made transferable by endorsement, and those notes of less than $100 bore no interest at all and were payable to bearer. This was the first Honest Money issued by the Congress of the United States which did not pay interest to the usurer.

Thirteenth Congress, Sess. III., Chap. 56, Feb. 24th, 1815.

An Act to authorize the issuing of Treasury notes for the service of the year, one thousand eight hundred and fifteen (a).

Sec. 3. And be it further enacted, That the said Treasury notes shall be prepared of such denominations as the secretary of the Treasury, with the approbation of the President of the United States, shall from time to time direct ; and such of the said notes as shall be of a denomination less than one hundred dollars, shall be payable to bearer, and be transferable by delivery alone, and shall bear no interest ; and such of the said notes as shall be of the denomination of one hundred, or upwards, may be payable to order, and transferable by delivery and assignment, endorsed on the same, and bearing an interest from the day on which they shall be issued, at the rate of five and two-fifths per centum per annum ; or they may be made payable to bearer, and transferable by delivery alone, and bearing no interest, as the Secretary of the Treasury, with the approbation of the President of the United States, shall direct.

The above act called for the issue of $25,000,000. These notes were full legal tender for all debts, public and private, as the following section of the same Act shows :

Sec. 6. That the Treasury notes authorized to be issued by this Act, shall be everywhere receivable in all payments to the United States.

This $25,000,000 of paper money was made a full legal tender for all debts public and private, it was issued in a time when the country was in need because then this country was at war with England, which with a flottilla of sixty war ships had entered the Chesapeake Bay, captured Washington and burned the Capitol, really it was the first good service of paper money, and an example which ought to show that when paper money does the work in time of war and in time of need to a country, why it should not do the work at all time?

What is money and how it is made the framers of our Constitution put the words thus: Congress shall have power to "coin money." The words "coin money" was intended by the framers to mean make; then comes the words "and regulate the value thereof," which was intended, and it is the law, and it does not make a particle of difference of what material money is made of. A dollar is what the law of the United States makes a dollar, and so on with the francs of France and Italy, and the pound of England, etc. There is no such thing as standard of value. Supply and demand in open market makes prices, so it is the laws passed that make gold more valuable. Demonetize gold or do not use it as money, and it will depreciate in value as a commodity, sure.

Good, honest paper money always does the work. Now, it was with that money that our forefathers fought against the oppressor *octopus* that was annihilated and defeated by General Jackson at New Orleans. After the *octopus* has been whipped for the second time, she goes to work, knowing that she could not whip us by force, but proceeds to belittle us by schemes, and is succeeding in doing it right along now-a-days; and those psuedo or false American patriots are asleep or fail to wake up and govern their country without any advice from England. Are they observing the wishes and orders of England, or what are they doing?

Now, let us see if England did not do it, as she is doing it now, too; and the Gold Conspiracy of 1856 was not well planned. Let us prove it. In 1857–58–59 they commenced the tinkering with the Tariff and lessened the revenue of the government.

The President was in with the gang and depleting the treasury, as is being done now. While the *Octopus's* missionaries—politicians, etc.—were at work with the North and the South, the slave and secession questions were creating sectional hate, like now in the East, the South and West. The reader certainly recollects the election of that greatest American that ever was born, Honest Abe Lincoln, and the commencement of the War of the Rebellion for the benefit of the money sharks of Lombard street, London, and their Wall street, New York, associates. Buchanan had dispatched all our navy to Southern ports and not a cent in the treasury; the South had been instigated and promised with help, and did strike the blow. The country was declared at war. *Now*, we all know that war means money, because without money [medium of exchange] to procure the necessaries of life and ammunition for the soldiers to fight with, you could not fire a gun or swing a sword. Money means interest, when you have to borrow it. Interest means usury and usury means the final enslavement of the people—that they planned—no more Southern black slaves to King Cotton, but

NORTH AND SOUTH

Blacks and Whites, slaves to King Gold. The firing on Fort Sumter from Fort Morton forced President Lincoln to preserve the Union and not to divide and weaken the greatest nation on the face of the earth, and not to be split in two by the Gold Lords' schemes and have a perpetual feud (so the whipped *octopus* could come over and get revenge) and so President Lincoln was forced to ask August Belmont, an *octopus* or Rothschild defended banker of New York, to negotiate a loan for the government from the Rothschilds. What was the "Shylock's" answer? If he gives us a bond bearing a very high rate of interest, payable in gold interest and capital, and the bond to be based on the resources of the American people (which were and are yet better than any gold, but the Americans do not know that) we will lend him our gold. That was the answer sent to President Lincoln, the man of the common people (too honest a man for the rest) that refused to bond the country in a time of need and not like it is now, bonding it in a time of no need. A bond bearing a high rate of interest and based on the resources of

my people! No, said Lincoln, we will issue another piece of
paper and call it treasury notes (or greenbacks) and pay no
interest at all. The President was an American at that time,
one of the greatest patriotic Americans ever born (he was
assassinated for the lost cause, was he?) and he called the
attention of Congress and Senate and used his influence to
carry out the words and meaning of our Constitution,
Section VIII (8) Article V (5), and on July 17th, 1861, the
Secretary of the Treasury was authorized to issue 50 millions
of dollars of treasury notes (same money as in 1812–1815) the
best and most honest money ever issued, that saved the Union
and our country the second time when in need, and paid no
interest to Shylocks, and after it was made a full legal tender
for all debts, public and private, on March 17, 1862, reached
5 per cent premium over gold, and by said law of March 17,
1862, that made that currency a full legal tender for all debts,
public and private, the Shylock Bankers of Europe were
scared to death and commenced hallooing "Help" "au
Secours," "Hilf" "Help" "Help." What shall become

of our gold, asking the Wall street Bankers to help them, as
they saw Lincoln was coining money based on the resources

2

of the people that he was serving, and had no use for their gold. Here is the act that scared them:

Thirty-seventh Congress, Sess. I., Chap. 5, July 17, 1861:

An Act to authorize a National loan and for other purposes.
Proviso, post, p. 313.

The last four lines of Section 1 of said Act reads as follows:

And, *provided further*, That no Treasury notes shall be issued of less denomination than ten dollars, and that the whole amount of Treasury notes, not bearing interest, issued under authority of this Act, shall not exceed fifty millions of dollars.

Here we are again with fifty million dollars of honest money. The usurers of Europe called on their Wall Street friends to stop this and the latter immediately commenced to fix things for the stopping of Lincoln's example.

THEIR FIRST DIRTY WORK.

Thirty-seventh Congress, Sess. I., Chap. 46, Aug. 5, 1861:

An Act supplementary to an Act, entitled "An Act to authorize a National loan and for other purposes."

That the Secretary of the Treasuary is hereby authorized to issue bonds of the United States, bearing interest at six per centum per annum, and payable at the pleasure of the United Sates after twenty years from date, and if any holder of Treasury notes, bearing interest at the rate of seven and three-tenths per centum, which may be issued under authority of the Act to authorize a National loan and for other purposes, approved July seventeenth, eighteen hundred and sixty-one, shall desire to exchange the same for bonds, the Secretary of Treasury may at any time before or at the maturity of the said notes, issue to said holder in payment thereof an amount of said bonds equal to the amount, which at the time of such payment or exchange, may be due on said Treasury notes ; but no such bonds shall be issued for a less sum than five hundred dollars, nor shall the whole amount of such bonds exceed the whole amount of Treasury notes not bearing seven and three-tenths per centum interest, issued under said Act ; and any part of the Treasury notes payable on demand authorized by said Act, may be made payable by the Assistant Treasurer at St. Louis, or depositories at Cincinnati.

Who would, as a matter of business, exchange notes drawing 7 and 3–10ths per cent. interest for bonds drawing 6 per cent. interest? Would you? Of course not. This aet was intended and aimed at other game. The object being to collect the $50,000,000 of non-interest bearing demand notes (issued under prior act, July 17, 1861), from the old soldiers and other citizens, and convert them into *interest bearing bonds*. The money-changers' *Agents* were collecting the demand notes, and for this reason, they had this supplementary act passed. Furthermore, you will notice that no bonds were to be issued for less amounts than $500. Why? Because it was to deprive the people with less amounts of money than $500 from obtaining any Bonds, and thereby be prevented from drawing interest, also to give the bankers the monopoly of exchanging the *non*-interest bearing demand notes for interest bearing bonds. Was it not a great money-making scheme to start with? How many old soldiers could invest $500 in bonds? The above demand notes were full legal tender for all dues.

SEC. 5. And be further enacted, That the Treasury notes (authorized by the Act to which this is supplementary) of a less denomination than fifty dollars, payable on demand, without interest, and not exceeding in amount the sum of fifty millions of dollars, shall be receivable in payment of all dues.

Another step taken by the conspirators to carry out their plans to control the currency of the country was to induce the Secretary of the Treasury to recommend the passage of the National Banking Act.

In December, 1861, Salmon P. Chase, then Secretary of the Treasury, in his annual report advocated a hybrid bill for the issuing of National Bank-notes, secured by a pledge of United States stocks, to take the place of State currency. He claimed it would create a currency of uniform value and diminish exchange and distribute the money so as to avoid monopoly.

The President was opposed to the Secretary's plan, so no effort was made for the time being, to frame a bill carrying out the Secretary's above recommendation.

The *conspirators* then changed their plans and induced the State banks to suspend specie payment, which the latter did on Dec. 31, 1861, and by such suspension and the distressed financial condition of the country forced a change and a new policy on the part of the administration, and the bankers having secured the services of Secretary Chase, the Secretary asked Congressman Spaulding of New York to present a National Bank Bill in Congress, but such was the opposition to it that it never was reported by the committee to whom it was referred in 1862. Three hundred millions of treasury notes were authorized to be issued; these were made legal tender for all debts, except government duties (the exception clause scheme that you will see the result of further on in this book).

TEN MILLIONS MORE OF HONEST MONEY ISSUED.

Thirty-seventh Congress, Sess. II., Chap. 20, Feb. 12, 1862:

An Act to authorize an additional issue of United States Treasury notes. That the Secretary of the Treasury, in *addition* to the fifty millions of notes payable on demand, of the denomination not less than five dollars, heretofore authorized by Acts of July seventeen and August fifth, eighteen hundred and sixty-one, be and he is hereby authorized to issue like notes, and for like purposes, to the amount of ten million dollars, and said notes shall be deemed part of the loan of two hundred and fifty millions of dollars. Approved Feb. 12, 1862.

NOW COMES THE MOST DISHONEST ACT

ever passed by the representatives of this government, an act which shows on its face the dishonesty on the part of the government against its people, an Act passed for the purpose of obtaining the products of the people's labor with a dishonest currency. (Obtaining goods under false pretences.)   An Act, the effect of which was to give the law-protected usurers the opportunity of becoming millionairs out of the cruel war, planned, started and prolonged by the *shylock usurers* of the world.

To think that the Congress of the United States passing an Act for the issuing of dishonest money (depreciated currency), to take up and retire the honest money (full legal tender notes). This seems impossible, but nevertheless it is true.   Oh, corrupt! venal! fraudulent deceivers of represenatives of a government of the people, for the people and by the people, passing a law to depreciate its own money by refusing to accept it back in payment of duties.

(The exception clause on the Government Treasury notes, or more correctly speaking, the greenbacks.) This law was passed for the benefit of the shylocks who were too cowardly to risk their miserable carcasses on the field of battle.

This law gave these stay-at-home Shylocks and Usurers the opportunity to purchase the Greenbacks at 50 cents on the dollar, and then (being allowed by a prior act) to convert these greenbacks into interest-bearing bonds (mortgages on the whole people), and thereby further enrich themselves.

Following is the Act which put the dishonest exception clause on the greenbacks (thereby causing them to fall in value to 50 cents on the dollar). The soldier received these greenbacks as his pay for risking his life on the battle-field, then he had to discount them to the banker, who changed these non-interest bearing greenbacks into interest bearing bonds, the latter at the same time receiving the double profit of being paid 100 cents on the dollar, besides the premium on the bonds when they were redeemed by the government, also a big interest on the bonds for many years. Which is it more profitable to be, a patriotic Soldier, or a stay-at-home Shylock? Which one does the government take the most care of? To one it gives a few dollars a month pension, to the other, millions of money, as interest and premium on bonds.

HERE IS THE ACT.

Thirty-seventh Congress, Sess. II., Chap. 33, Feb. 25th, 1862:

An Act to authorize the issue of United States Notes, and for the redemption or funding thereof of the floating debt of the United States.

Be it enacted by the Senate and House of Representatives of the United States of America in Congress assembled. That the Secretary of the Treasury is hereby authorized to issue, on the credit of the United States, one hundred and fifty millions of dollars of United States notes not bearing interest, and of such denominations as he may deem expedient. not less than five dollars each. *Provided, however, that fifty millions of said notes shall be in lieu of the demand treasury notes, authorized to be issued by the act of July seventeen, eighteen hundred and sixty one, which said demand notes shall be taken up as rapidly as practicable, and the notes herein provided for substituted for them,* and provided further, That the amount of the *two kinds* of notes together shall at no time exceed the sum of one hundred and fifty millions of dollars, and such notes herein authorized shall be receivable in payment of all taxes, internal duties, excises, debts and demand of every kind due to the United States. *Except duties on imports* and all claims and demands against the United States of every kind whatsoever, *except for interest upon the bonds and notes, which shall be paid in coin,* and shall also be lawful money and a legal tender in payment of all debts public and private within the United States, *except duties on imports and interest aforesaid.* And that holder of said United States notes depositing any sum not less than fifty dollars, or some multiple of fifty dollars, with the Treasurer of the United States or either of the Assistant Treasurers, shall receive in exchange therefor duplicate certificates of deposit, one of which may be transmitted to the *Secretary of the Treasury, who shall thereupon issue to the holder an equal amount of bonds of the United States, coupon or registered, as may be, by said holder, be desired, bearing interest at the rate of six per centum per annum, payable semi annually,* and redeemable at the pleasure of the United States after five years, and payable twenty years from the date thereof, and such United States notes shall be received the same as coin, at the par value in payment for any loans that may be hereafter sold or negotiated by the Secretary of the Treasury, and may be re-issued from time to time as the exigencies of the public interest shall require.

Lincoln was compelled to approve this Act, because he wanted to end the rebellion and stop a murderous war. The Secretary of the Treasury, Salmon P. Chase and all the Bankers used their influence with Lincoln, telling him that this was the only way to make the foreign importers pay their duties in Gold. You will notice that $50,000,000 of those notes with the exception clause on them, were to take up and retire the greenbacks which had no exception clause on, thereby putting the merchants and citizens who had to pay duties on imports at the mercy of the gold bugs, who charged extortionate premiums for their gold. The merchants and citizens were forced to accept these greenbacks in payment for their goods or labor, as they were made legal tender for any claim against the government; also being lawful money and a legal tender for all debts, public and private, except *duties on imports and interest on bonds.* A continual chain was thus formed for the re-issue of these notes. The government paying them to the soldiers and citizens in settlement of claims against it, and they in turn being compelled to discount them to the gold banker, who got the government to change these greenbacks into interest bearing bonds. This interest was payable every six months in coin, which gave the bankers the chance of getting the gold back again, thus keeping in motion the greatest robbing scheme ever conceived by the brain of man, and they keep it in motion at the present time, as the exception clause yet remains on the greenbacks, bank notes, etc. No wonder that the bankers became millionaires! And they intend to grow richer and richer by continuing in the future this scheme of making the people pay extortionate premium on gold. How long? Oh! how long will it be before the great and intelligent (?) people of America, wake up from their dreams and realize how they are robbed.

Sec. 2. Same Act.

And be it further enacted, That the Secretary of the Treasury to fund the Treasury notes and floating debt of the United States, he is hereby authorized to issue, on the credit of the United States, coupon bonds, or registered bonds to an amount not exceeding five hundred millions of dollars, redeemable at the pleasure of the United States after five years, and payable twenty years from date and bearing interest at the rate of six per centum per annum, payable semi-annually, and the bonds herein authorized shall be of such denominations, not less than fifty dollars, as may be determined upon by the Secretary of the Treasury, and the Secretary of the Treasury may dispose of such bonds at any time, at the market value thereof, for coin of the United States, or for any Treasury notes that have been or may hereafter be issued under any former Act of Congress, or for United States notes that may be issued under the provisions of this Act, and all stocks, bonds and other securities of the United States held by individuals, corporations or associations within the United States shall be exempt from taxation by or under State's authority.

BANKER SELLING THE GOLD

PERSON WHO PAYS THE DUTIES IN GOLD

UNCLE SAM RETURNING THE GOLD TO THE BANKER

How the Exception Clause on the currency worked during the War and works now. It takes six months for the Gold to get back to the Banker again by the continuous chain scheme.

You see that *no taxes* are paid by the Bond-holder on their bonds, and the Bond Sharks are now growling at the Silver Lunatics (?) because the latter want silver remonetized so that the government will find it easier to pay the bonds and lighten the people's burden; saying that, "they want to ruin the country." Touch a man's pocket-book and he will squeal. By the foregoing Act the people of the United States were robbed of *two billions, one hundred and ten millions of dollars ;* or, in other words, the farmers and laboring people of this country paid to the bankers $2,110,000,000 as interest on an original debt of $500,-000,000, or more than four times as much interest than what the principal amounted to.

See illustration of farmer, storekeeper and banker. You can figure it out yourself.

Following is an Act, passed by the tools of the money-lenders, authorizing the Secretary of the Treasury to purchase coin with any of the bonds, or other notes of the United States. This is the Act which King(?) Grover the First! (elected as Presi-dent), had his J. G. Carlisle quote as authority for the issue of the $62,500,000 bonds, of February, 1895, using the proceeds of the same to pay the current expenses of the government, not knowing that there is an Act on the Statute Books of the United States, approved April 13, 1866, forbidding the increase of the public debt :

Thirty–seventh Congress, Sess. II., Chap. 45, March 17, 1862 :

An Act to authorize the purchase of coin and for other purposes.

SEC. 1. That the Secretary of the Treasury may purchase coin with any of the bonds or notes of the United States authorized by law, at such rates and upon such terms as he deems most advantageous to the public interest ; and may issue, under such rules and regulations as he may prescribe, certificates of indebtedness, such as are authorized by an Act entitled : "An Act to authorize the Secretary of the Treasury to issue certificates of indebtedness to public creditors." Approved March first, eighteen hundred and sixty-two, to such creditors as may desire to re-ceive the same.

Demand notes made a full legal-tender for all purposes, by Section two of this Act.

SEC. 2. And be it further enacted, That the demand notes authorized by the Act of July seventeen, eighteen hundred and sixty-one, and by the Act of Feb-ruary twelfth, eighteen hundred and sixty-two, shall, in addition to being receivable in payment of duties on imports, be receivable and shall be lawful money and a legal tender, in like manner and for the same purposes, and to the same extent, as the notes authorized by an Act entitled, "An Act to authorize the issue of United States notes, and for the redemption or funding thereof, and for funding the float-ing debt of the United States." Approved February twenty-fifth, eighteen hun-dred and sixty-two.

By the Act just quoted the $60,000,000 of demand notes, issued under the two former Acts, were made a full legal tender for all debts, public and private, duties on imports, interest on the public debt (Honest Money). They were appreciated in value and went to a premium of *five per cent. above gold.*

Why did not Congress make all the notes full legal tender? If it had done so, no interest bearing bonds would have been necessary, and no robbery of the people committed.

Thirty-seventh Congress, Sess. II., July 11, 1862:

Authorizing the issue of $150,000,000 Treasury notes not bearing interest.

Was there a Gold Conspiracy or not?

Now, let us see ; it was that paper money, and not coward gold that runs away in time of need, that was paid to the soldiers fighting to save the Union on the battlefields, and the reader will certainly recollect that in the latter part of the Summer of 1862, the South was nearly whipped, as the Monitor had sunk the Merrimac, and General Grant had captured Fort Donaldson, and the Civil War would have surely come to an end if it were not for the Shylock money lenders of Lombard street, London, and Wall street, N. Y., that were working to have it prolonged, so as to get their work in. Let us follow the result. The copperhead element was interfering and holding the hands of the President to prolong the war, and that was what the Bankers wanted to work ; that eventful Fall Election for Congressmen was held, and now you see the greatest Italian hand ever played in the history of this country during that eventful Fall Election. The Bankers carried their plan by electing their tools to prolong the war, also had the outgoing Congressmen so scared or fixed that they passed the vicious National Banking Law, which had failed to be passed before.

As soon as this Congress met the Secretary of the Treasury and all the Bankers' lobbyists commenced to work to secure the passage of a law which is so partial and that gives a certain class of citizens (the rich and moneyed citizens) the advantage over other poor citizens, just as good or even better, for that matter, because the writer considers the farmer and producers the backbone of any country. Suppose the latter would stop seeding, where would the Bankers and the country be?

Let us observe the result!

In Dec., 1862, the Secretary of the Treasury (same Chase) in his report of said date, again called attention to his National Bank scheme, and called attention to the danger arising from the issue of United States notes and claimed great advantages by using the National Bank notes, the bankers having had plenty of time to fix things had Congress interested and took up the Spaulding Bill in the House of Representatives. Now the bankers did not like the Spaulding Bill in the shape it was, and engaged Senator Sherman, "Honest John" of Ohio, whom they retained for a long while (and may have him yet) to amend the bill introduced in the House, and on Jan. 26th, 1863, in the Senate, Mr. Sherman asked and by unanimous consent obtained leave to bring in a Bill (S. No. 486) to provide a National currency secured by a pledge of the United States stocks and to provide for the circulation and redemption thereof, which was read twice by its title.

Mr. Sherman "I will state with the leave of the Senate that there are some features of the Bill a 'little' different from the Bill introduced in the House of Representatives. I do not know that it is necessary to print it until it is reported back from the Committee of Finance, but at the suggestion of some Senators, I will move that it be printed and referred to the Committee on Finance." The Bill was ordered printed and referred to the Committee, and Mr. Sherman, watched carefully, and debated hours and hours for his Bill. (See Sherman's remarks on Currency, Congressional Records pages 505, 666, 703, 820, 840, 869, 1155, 1235, 1237, 1306, it will astonish you the fight he made for this Bill) and finally came to a vote in the Senate on Feb. 12, 1863, and was passed by a small majority. Senator Trumbull of Illinois a Republican and a friend of Lincoln and Grimes of Ia. fought it to the last.

Thirty-seventh Congress, Sess. III., Chap. 58, Feb. 25, 1863:

An Act to provide a National currency, secured by a pledge of United States stocks, and to provide for the circulation and redemption thereof. That there shall be established in the Treasury Department a separate bureau, which shall be charged with the execution of this law, and all other laws that may be passed by Congress respecting the issue and regulation of a National currency secured by United States bonds. The chief officer of said bureau shall be denominated the

Comptroller of the Currency, and shall be under the general direction of the Secretary of the Treasury, he shall be appointed by the President on the nomination of the Secretary of the Treasury, by and with the advice and consent of the Senate and shall hold his office for the term of five years, unless removed by the President by and with the consent of Senate.

This first section continues in regard to the comptroller's duties, which it is not material to publish here. The following are the most *important* sections of the *National Banking Act.* " United States Bonds " to mean what?

SEC. 4.   And be it enacted, that the term " United States Bonds " as used in this Act, shall be construed to mean all coupon and registered bonds now issued or that may hereafter be issued on the faith of the United States by the Secretary of the Treasury in pursuance of law.

SEC. 5.   That associations for carrying on the business of banking may be formed by any number of persons ; not less in any case than five.

SEC. 6.   That persons uniting to form such an association, shall, under their hand and seal, make certificate which shall specify—

First.—The name assumed by such association.

Second.—The place where its operations of discount and deposit are to be carried on ; designating the State, Territory or District, and also the particular city, town or village.

Third.—The amount of its capital stock and the number of shares into which the same shall be divided ; which capital stock shall not be less than fifty thousand dollars ; and in cities whose population is over ten thousand persons, the capital stock shall not be less than one hundred thousand dollars.

According to this last section it proves that this law was passed to enable the rich to have a monopoly of the *banking* business. How many old soldiers or citizens were or are able to raise even the minimum, $50,000, in order to start a *National Bank.* As that amount is still the limit fixed by the law, who gets the benefit of the law, the masses of the people or the rich classes? The mercenary editors of the great dailies, owned body, soul and conscience by this latter class, dare not tell the truth or disclose this gigantic robbery of the people, committed by the law-protected banking brigands. This banking system threatens the destruction of this American Republic.

SEC. 15.   That every association, after having complied with the provisions of this Act, preliminary to the commencement of the banking business under these provisions, shall transfer and deliver to the Treasurer of the United States any United States bonds bearing interest to an amount not less than one-third of the capital stock paid in ; which bonds shall be deposited with the Treasurer of the United States and by him safely kept in his office until the same shall be otherwise disposed of, in pursuance of the provision of this Act.

You see the kindness of the law-makers towards the rich bond-holding bankers. They built them great vaults and safe deposits, so that they can keep their bonds, guarded at public expense from thieves, fire or water, and the government does not charge them a cent for taking care of them. Blessed are the rich, for they shall own the earth and everybody on it.

SEC. 16. That upon the making of any such transfer and delivery, the association making the same shall be entitled to receive from the Comptroller of the Currency, circulating notes of different denominations in blank, registered and countersigned as hereinafter provided, equal in amount to ninety per centum of the current market value of the United States bonds, so transferred and delivered, but not exceeding the par value thereof if bearing interest at the rate of six per centum.

Did you ever hear of a business man who, paying interest on his debts, allows his creditor to issue 90 per cent. *more* notes of credit, based upon the strength of the first man's debts, so that the aforesaid creditor could lend these notes back to the debtor (or other persons), and thereby get more interest out of the debtor. Well! he was crazy, if you ever did hear of him? That, though, is exactly what the intelligent (?) law-makers allowed the *bankers* to do when they passed the *National Banking Act.* Yet the Republican party calls this sound financiering, and the father of the Act they call Honest John. That Act has created millionairs and tramps. How many of each you can best judge for yourself. The people have paid millions of dollars interest on bonds during the past thirty-three years, and are still paying interest. Issuing money on the strength of debts is the last thing that any one ever expected to hear of, but such is the case with the United States of America.

What great political economists and financiers (for their own pockets), these American law-makers were.

Here is the vote on this bill :

YEAS.

Messrs. Anthony, Arnold, Chandler, Clark, Dolittle, Fessenden, Foster, Harding, Harlan, Harris, Howard, Howe, Lane of Kansas, Morril, Nesmith, Pomeroy, " *Sherman,*"

Sumner, Ten Eyek, Wade, Wilkinson, Wilmot, and Wilson of Massachusetts (23).

NAYS.

Messrs. Carlisle, Collamer, Cowan, Davis, Dixon, Foot, Grimes, Henderson, Hiks, Kennedy, King, Latham, McDougall, Powel, Rice, Richards, Saulsbury, Trumbul, Turpie, Wall, and Wilson of Missouri (21). So the Bill was passed. The President signed it Feb. 25th, 1863 (as Chase had said to him that he would resign as Secretary of the Treasury within two hours if the President would veto the Bill). This is what is called the National Banking Law, but another Act was passed on June 3rd, 1864, creating National Banks, the latter being a substitute act.

Now is this a country of equal rights to all and privilege to none?

Let us see! According to the above laws a National Banker can go and buy a bond, say of $100,000, pay for it in gold, then take it to the Secretary of the Treasury for deposit and receive $90,000 in greenbacks, or authority to issue $90,000 in bank notes just as good as gold to buy anything with. Now how much does it leave that the banker invested? Only $10,000, and he gets interest on $100,000 and pays no tax, as the law says that government bonds are non-taxable. Then he lends the $90,000, say at 10 per cent, and in a year he has again $100,000 to buy another bond, you know, and so on to get interest on what they owe.

Let us see how it works on another citizen or set of citizens. He can go and buy a bond, say of $100,000 (if the administration does not do as it did with the Stewart & Co. trust—all $50,000,000 or none) then he takes that bond to Uncle Sam's Treasury for deposit and asks for the $90,000 that the banker got for his bond. The Secretary of the Treasury says to him "You must be a National Banker." The citizen gets excited and tells Uncle Sam that this is a country of equal rights to all and privilege to none, and he has to have the $90,000 as he needs the amount to help to carry out his enterprise. Uncle Sam says to him that he would like to accommodate him but he cannot do it as the

Law of Feb. 25th, 1863, stops him. The citizen gets angry and says that Law is a Steel Trap, with accent on the "Steel" to catch us in. Uncle Sam gets mad and says "What, sir, it is your own fault, you have been sending men here to legislate for you for the last twenty-five or thirty years, and they are ruining my farms and taking all my products to Europe for nothing, but I tell you that I am here to fulfil the law," and hands him the law. Now, no matter what the other citizen would do with the $90,000 if he got it—start a factory or plantation, or improve his property so that it would furnish labor and increase wealth in the country, he has to invest $100,000, while the banker only has to invest $10,000. Is that law that "Honest John" introduced and passed, Just? No! certainly not.

BANKER   CITIZEN

National Banking law and how it works. One gets greenbacks the other the Law.

WIIAT A NATIONAL BANKER CAN DO.

Here is what a national banker can do with $150,000 in gold. First, he buys $100,000 worth of bonds, then deposits the bonds with the Secretary of the Treasury and receives $90,000 in national bank notes. With these he buys products of labor (cotton, corn or wheat) and then sells the latter in Europe for gold. With this gold and $10,000 of the $50,000 he buys another $100,000 bond, takes out more bank notes, etc. He repeats this operation five times, when the $50,000 is all used. The banker will then, by these operations, be the owner of a half million of untaxable interest-bearing bonds; he will also be the possessor of $90,000 in bank notes, and it is possible for the national banker to keep doing this as long as the Government continues to issue bonds. You will observe that the national banker, by the above operations, increased his wealth $440,000 by the advantages given him by this most vicious banking act.

Let us see what another citizen can do by working the same way with, say, a $100,000: Buy a bond, take it to the Secretary of the Treasury for deposit and ask for the $90,000 greenbacks or authority to issue notes on the strength of his bond, the Secretary of the Treasury will say to him you must be a national banker.

The citizen will say:

What, Sir! This is a country of equal rights to all and privileges to none.

U. S. Treasurer—That is not true, Sir! The bankers now have all the privileges which they want, and will see to it that they are continued from now on.

Citizen—I must have $90,000. I need it to carry on my enterprises.

Treasurer—I told you, Sir, that you must be a pet national banker to get it, according to the law. What do I care about your enterprises?

Citizen—Well, you have disregarded the coinage laws and paid the Government obligations in gold when you should have paid them in coin. Silver coin, I mean. So you can disregard this banking law, which is a steel trap, with the accent on the "steel," and give me the $90,000.

TREASURER—Say! don't you dare talk that way to me. That banking law was introduced by a great financier and a friend of mine. He is a Republican, but that does not matter. We agree on what is good for us and fool the people on party lines, but there is no difference between us on this subject, so you had best refrain from talking about him and the law. Here it is, read it for yourself.

CITIZEN—I do not care to read that law again, because it is the worst law on the statute books, and the man who introduced and had it passed is a traitor and a disgrace to the people of America, and such laws are a menace to the people's liberties. Give me the $90,000 and do not force me to say any more on the subject.

TREASURER—Young man, you had better be careful what you say about my friend. He is backed by the richest men in the country. Go away from here. I cannot give you the $90,000. You must be crazy to ask for it.

CITIZEN—Do not make any threats about my getting into trouble. What for? Telling the truth? You people holding office claim to know all about the financial question (or any other question for that matter) when, in reality, you know nothing at all about it, only what your masters, the Rothschilds and Morgans, make you believe, and do. Give me the $90,000. I need it to carry on my business. As for your advice, keep it for your own use.

TREASURER—Porter, call an officer and have this man removed. He is crazy and wants $90,000. The law of February 25th, 1863, was not introduced for crazy people like him. It was passed for the benefit of the favorite few (the rich). Be quick. Get the officer and have him lock this man up as a lunatic.

. CITIZEN—That is what cowardly officers of the people like you do, turn over to the police as crazy a citizen that defends his rights granted to him by the Constitution.

The citizen had to withdraw or get arrested. He does not receive the $90,000 which the banker would have received had the latter asked for it.

An answer in advance. Now they will say this is a free country, and you can do the same thing, start a National Bank and have the same privilege. Oh, yes, it does not take much to start a National Bank, only $50,000 is the lowest limit of the law. How many American citizens can raise that much—so small a sum you find it in everybody's pocket in these days, don't you? But suppose that every citizen had $50,000 and all went banking, wouldn't this be a great country, we would live high on looking at money, but who would produce the wealth and necessaries of life?

No wonder bankers can afford to build ten and twenty story buildings (See illustration, City of Bankers' country).

NOW COMES THE TROUBLE.

The cruel war has come to an end and the bankers have farmed Uncle Sam's notes, and they cannot pay them back to him as duties, as they are marked on the back, and Lincoln will not now bond the country in time of peace, as he refused to bond it in time of war and in need. He would use his power and influence to not bond the country and his people that he loved so well, and he was a fearless man and did not hesitate a moment to fearlessly express his opinion on the subject, and at the end of the war when his friend in Springfield, Ill., wrote him congratulating him that he had brought the civil war to an end, he answered "Yes, the civil war is at an end, but I see a power going into Congress through party prejudice worse than all the armies of the South, for the enslavement of my people (how prophetically he spoke). As to the stand he took against the Wall street gold sharks, we all know it. He would never have taken any banker's advice.

Lincoln foresaw a bad future as a result of the war, and predicts the destruction of the republic. Here is what he said when the war was nearing its end:

"Yes; we may all congratulate ourselves that this cruel war is nearing a close. It has cost a vast amount of blood and treasure. The best blood of the flower of American youth has been freely offered upon our country's altar that the nation might live. It has been, indeed, a trying hour for the Republic, *but I see in the near future a crisis approaching that unnerves me and causes me to tremble for the safety of my country.* As a result of the war *corporations have been enthroned* and an era of *corruption in high places* will follow and the *money power* of the country will endeavor to *prolong its reign by working* upon the *prejudices* of the people until the *wealth is aggregated in a few hands* and the *Republic is destroyed. I feel* at this *moment more anxiety* for the *safety of my country* than ever before, even in the midst of war. *God grant* that my suspicion may prove groundless."

Great Scott! what a prophet. The far-reaching mind of Lincoln foresaw the coming events. The seed of a gigantic plant had been planted on the foundation of the war by a class who intended to take care of it, develop its growth and not allow it to die. The money power is doing its best to keep it growing. Lincoln predicted its growth and was preparing his rail-splitting axe to chop it off. But it would have been better for him and for the country if he had not said anything about the money power tree, for then he might have been living yet to-day if natural death had not called him. This and other actions of the Honest President put the conspirators' plant in danger if Lincoln had lived. Let us follow the result:

THE ASSASSINATION OF LINCOLN. WHY?

The true secret of the assassination of President Lincoln has never before been written. Many people believe that it was for the *Lost Cause*, while others think that religion had something to do with it. At any rate it is the concensus of public opinion, that Lincoln's assassination was the much to be deplored, successful execution of a deliberate conspiracy, to either kill or kidnap the martyred President. Now, who could be benefitted by his death, and who were the persons behind the scenes of this conspiracy? It is well known that Lincoln was bitterly opposed to the bonding of this country, and to the financial policy, of which certain leaders in Congress were only the mouthpieces. The persons who would profit most, were the ones who most desired his death, because he was honest and opposed their schemes.

Let us be reasonable and carefully consider this matter. Neither religion nor the Lost Cause could have profitted by the death of Lincoln. He was no religious bigot, and he had no animosity against the South. Lee had surrendered and the war between the North and South was ended. In fact his assassination was a great injury to the South, because it led to the reconstruction times, which injured the South more than the war had done. Many Southern leaders have said, "that in the death of Lincoln the South lost her best friend." In the Funding Act of 1866, the Credit Strengthing Act of 1869, the Refunding Act of 1870 and the crime of 1873 (which legislation, Lincoln's policy was opposed to), we see a chain of evidence which shows who were really benefitted by the death of Lincoln. Besides this, the writer will now disclose and make public, after four years research and investigation, and after having been convinced, the true reasons why Lincoln was assassinated.

In February, 1891, while in business in Los Angeles, California, I made the acquaintance of one Felippo Froscari, with whom I had some business dealings and who got into my debt. He left Los Angeles, saying that he would be gone about two months and would return with plenty of money, but refused to say where he was going. On his return he said that he had not found the party from whom he had expected to receive the money; and was greatly disappointed, for a previous occasion he had been away for about three months and returned with $15,000, to my certain knowledge, as can also be certified by James Castruccio, an Italian merchant, at No. 30 North Main street, Los Angeles, Cal., and others who knew Froscari. Shortly afterwards Froscari died in the Venezia House, a small boarding place kept by a Venetian named Gætano Lissari. Before his death he told me that, in consideration of my kindness to him, he would reveal to me a secret that might be of benefit if I wanted to make it public. He said:

"My real name is not Felippo Froscari. It is Arthur Borghese. I committed a wrong in Rome and my relatives, who are rich, sent me to London to escape arrest. There I went by the name of Arditi. Being followed, I left there for Montreal, Canada, where I made the acquaintance of John Wilkes Booth, the man who later killed Lincoln. He was very generous to everybody, and especially to me, and several times insisted on giving me money, although I was not in need of it. At his request I went with him to New York, where he promised that if I would not betray his secrets and would co-operate with him, he would insure me wealth for my life-time. I swore on a cross and a Bible, and then he informed me that he had been to Canada to make arrangements with interested parties there to kill President Lincoln, because Lincoln was no good and dishonest. He showed me two London newspapers containing articles after Lincoln's re-election. I did not fancy harming a complete stranger to me, but he assured me that the country and the world at large would honor us, and seduced me by his promises of money.

I was paid a large sum immediately by him, which he got from a man who was to leave for London the next day. Booth and I went to Washington, D. C., but found no opportunity to assassinate Lincoln, so we went South, where I left Booth. Until now I have kept my secret, and only tell you because I am about to die.

The next day Froscari died. What he had said greatly impressed me, and I concluded to investigate the matter. I have spent considerable time and money in so doing. The following is strong and conclusive evidence, which I have collected to corroborate Froscari's statement, which, in my opinion, proves conclusively that Booth had been in Canada in consultation with English financiers before he assassinated Lincoln.

One year, less three days, from Lincoln's death, an Act called the Funding Act, was passed by Congress, by which Act the Bondholders ultimately made $2,110,000,000. Would Lincoln have signed such an act?

ENGLISH HATE AGAINST LINCOLN.

From the London Herald, organ of the English aristocrats, of November 22, 1864, after Mr. Lincoln's re-election:

* * * Mr. Lincoln has been re-elected. He will go on, in his own phrase, "pegging way," at objects already shown to be unattainable. Lincoln *is a vulgar, brutal boor*, wholly ignorant of political science, of military affairs, of everything else, which a statesman should know. He has allowed the public to be *robbed to an indefinite extent* by his ministers. He has shielded them from punishment, continued them in office, and in the only case in which the scandal was too bad to be hushed up at home, he appointed the guilty party to a first-class embassy. For our own part we rejoice that the cause of *oppression, robbery* and *injustice* is entrusted to the hands of a *vacillating, helpless imbecile* rather than to those of an able, resolute and efficient soldier (McClellan).

The London Standard and Globe were so venal in their vilification of Mr. Lincoln after his re-election that to not insult the memory of the Great President the writer will refrain to publish here what was printed by these two pimp and dude papers, which accused Mr. Lincoln as a *corrupt, dishonest brute,* and that the people of the North had been duped besides. Why all this, the readers can judge for themselves. Mr. Lincoln's policy was against England's Gold Standard Policy, and division of the country.

In the Century Magazine of January, 1890, appears an interesting article which was copyrighted in 1886 by John G. Nicolay and John Hay, Private Secretaries to President Lincoln.

Messrs. Nicolay and Hay state in their article (quoted below) on page 432, second column, that after Mr. Lincoln's re-election, Booth had visited Canada, here is what they say in speaking of Booth :

He visited Canada, consorted with the rebel emissaries there, and at last, whether or not at their instigation cannot certainly be said, conceived a scheme to capture the President and to take him to Richmond, he spent a great part of the Autumn and Winter, in inducing a small number of loose fish of Secession Sympathizers to join him in this fantastic enterprise. He seemed always well supplied with money, and talked largely of his speculations in oil as a source of income ; but his agent afterwards testified that he never realized a dollar from that source ; that his investments, which were inconsiderable, were a total loss. The Winter passed away, and nothing was accomplished. On the fourth of March Booth was at the Capitol and created a disturbance by trying to force his way through the line of policemen who guarded the passage through which the President walked to the east front of the building. His intentions at this time are not known ; he afterwards said he lost an excellent chance of killing the President that day. There are indications in the evidence given on the trial of the conspirators that they suffered some great disappointment in their schemes in the latter part of March, and a letter from Arnold to Booth, dated March 27, showed some of them had grown timid of consequences of their contemplated enterprise. He advised Booth, before going further, "to go and see how it will be taken in R—d."

In page 440 of same article Mr. Nicolay and Hay say that Congress did not conceal the gratification that Lincoln was no longer in their way. Here is their language in said article :

In a political caucus, held a few hours after the President's death, they resolved on an entire change of Cabinet, and a "line of policy less conciliatory than that of Mr. Lincoln, . . . the feeling was nearly universal." We are using the language of one of their most prominent representatives, "that the accession of Johnson to the Presidency would prove a godsend to the country."

The next day the committee on conduct of the war called on the new President, and Senator Wade bluntly expressed to him the feeling of his associates : "Johnson, we have faith in you. By the Gods, there will be no trouble now in running the government."

According to the statement made by Mr. Wade, Senator from Ohio, it shows that Mr. Lincoln had or would cause some trouble in carrying out some different plan than that subsequently put into operation by the currency contractionists.

In the end of Messrs. Nicolay's and Hays' article, on page 449, there is the report of Captain E. P. Dohorty, who had charge of the Twenty-fifth Cavalry, men that went after Booth. He states: That after Booth had died, he searched and found on him a draft on Canada for sixty pounds besides other things.

ABRAHAM LINCOLN (one of the victims).

We see that Lincoln had to be taken out of the way so that the conspirators could carry out their plan. What could the South gain by killing Lincoln? Nothing. The war was over. The South lost by the death of Lincoln. But it would do the conspirators great good. They could carry out their plans, which they did.

After his death, the bankers said to Uncle Sam your credit is running down with the notes you issued, and you had better fund your debt. On April 12th, 1866, the Funding Act was passed. On March 1st, 1869, the credit strengthening act was passed; no need for it, the credit of this nation was good. But the conspirators that had the refunding act in view, which was passed on July 24th, 1870, making the bonds payable in coin. Feb. 12th, 1873, the demonetizing of silver act was passed, with the influence of £100,000 ($500,000) English money, with orders to draw $500,000 more if necessary to carry out the instructions of the Bank of England and other European Bankers. This was also a scheme of "Honest John" and his honest Dollar. See sworn statement before the Clerk of the Supreme Court of the State of Colorado on page, 48 and Gold is King. Jan. 14th, 1875, resumption act was passed, giving the Secretary of the Treasury the power to issue bonds, and it is under this act that Secretary Carlisle has issued the $262,000,000 of new bonds. Sherman was Secretary of the Treasury at the time of the passage of the above act, but the act did not take effect until 1879. Jan. 12th, 1888, the Extended Bank Charter was passed and approved by the present Buzzard Bay fat Fisherman. 1890 the Sherman Silver Purchasing Act was passed, and Nov. 1st., 1893, the unconditional repeal of the said act by special request of President Cleveland, and the commencement of issuing more Government Bonds—1894, $100,000,000; 1895, $62,500,000; 1896, $100,-000,000 and more coming; 1897, ? and the conspiracy is complete and a success. The above laws are the reason for it and they were passed by the influence of the bankers (in evidence I quote John Sherman, before he became a Shylock in 1862). He said in the Senate "I much prefer the credit of the United States, based as it is upon all the production and properties of the United States to the issue of any corporation however well guarded and managed;" and after he became a Shylock, to wit: when Chairman of the Senate Finance Committee, on Dec. 12th, 1867, he said, "It was found necessary, that without the restriction upon the Greenbacks, the Bonds could not be negotiated, and it became necessary to depreciate the notes in order to create a market for the bonds."

Now here is an illustration, exactly the same with the government and the bankers.

We take a farmer, a store-keeper and a banker, we say in 1860, when there was need of currency. It is known that the farmer is considered always good; has a good farm and is out of debt, and he wishes to buy goods, say clothing, provisions, etc., to seed his farm, and agrees to issue his notes to the amount, say of $1,100 to the store-keeper for goods. The store-keeper is glad to get them, because he can pay his bills with them or buy the products back from the farmer and return the notes. The farmer needs $100 worth of goods and issues the first note to the merchant. Now the banker finds out that the farmer is giving the merchant notes and sends for the farmer and says to him " Why do you not put on the back of the note 'without recourse to me' before delivering the notes to the merchant," and tells him that in that way the merchant cannot bring the notes to the farmer but has to negotiate them with the banker (see the trap that the banker puts) and the farmer does it and finally delivers the notes to the merchant for the goods. Now the merchant wishes to go abroad or to California, and says to the banker (who has planned the trap) " I expect I had better get some gold to take with me, as they do not know John where I am going and would not take his notes." "Yes," the banker says, "We can accommodate you and take John's notes." So the store-keeper lays down $200 in John's notes and expects $200 in gold, less the discount that they agreed on. The banker takes the first note and says that it is all right, but the second one he looks at and then says " We cannot give you more than fifty cents on the dollar for it." The store-keeper kicks. " Why do you not see it has the exception clause on the back, what did you take it for?" It does no good, and he has to lay on another $100 note, giving two for one, for it has the exception clause on the back. Now the merchant goes and tries to pay some duty to the farmer and lays down the farmer's notes that he took for the goods he gave, and to his surprise the farmer says "They are no good, you will have to get gold to pay me the duty." " Why in the world did you give them to me if they are no good! You are a deceiver and false." " You had no business to take them" says the farmer, and so the merchant has to negotiate the notes with the banker at 40c. and 50c. on the dollar or less. This applies to poor old soldiers that fought and risked their lives in the war of the rebellion, that were paid with those kind of notes from farmer Uncle Sam. Think of it! Risking your life and then being deceived by the man that you protected, to give a chance to the banker to rob you, and the farm you defended he bonds afterwards for the full amount for twenty years, and does it now to please the bankers.

In the course of a little time, or at the end of the war, the banker has all the notes and sees the farmer again and tells him he had better fund his debt for his credit is running down you know. He does it, and gives a mortgage bond on the farm for $1,100 for 20 years at 5 per cent interest. The interest comes due the first year, and he gives his first note for $55. Second year, $58. Third year, $61., and at the end of twenty years he has given $1,771 (as interest alone) and he now owes $2,871, and the currency or the notes has been taken up and put into a mortgage. The debts must be paid in gold and nowhere to get it from except from the banker, or lose his farm that is worth $8,000 and cost the banker just a little over $500 in gold, to get $2,871 in a mortgage that must be paid in gold or all lost. $2,300 lost by taking the banker's advice (you think that when you pay a debt four times that you are out of the debt, but this way you owe yet more than the fellow loaned you).

Now let us see if that is not a parallel case to the action of the bankers with farmer Uncle Sam, or the government.

On July 17, 1861, a Bill (H. R. 14) in the Senate July 17, 1861. A message from the House announced that the Speaker had signed the following Bill, which thereupon received the signature of the vice-President. Bill (H. R. 14) to authorize a national loan and other purposes, authorizing the Secretary of the Treasury to issue $50,000,000 Treasury Notes. On March 17, 1862, Congress made $60,000,000 Treasury Notes full legal tender for all debts, public and private. The bankers then asked Congress to put on the back of the notes issued afterwards, the exception clause, which reads : "A full legal tender for all debts, public and private, except duties on imports and interest on the public debts." *Why* duties on imports ? Because it created and made a market for gold, and the citizen that had to pay the duties to the government (Uncle Sam) had to buy it from the bankers who sell it with their left hand and raise the price thereof. And why interest on the public debts ? Because it made the government (Uncle Sam) pay it back as interest on the bonds to the bondholders

(the bankers), who take it this time with their right hand so
as to be ready to sell it over again to some other citizen, thus
paying the duties and keep using it over and over again—the
same gold—from one hand to the other and make it scarce or
disappear when they want good prices for it, or force
Legislation, as they do now.

BANKER
SELLING
THE GOLD

PERSON
WHO PAYS
THE DUTIES
IN GOLD

UNCLE SAM
RETURNING
THE GOLD
TO THE
BANKER

The exception clause in our currency and how it
works; who gets the benefit.

Law of Feb. 25, 1863, the way it works: The exception
clause that yet exists on all the greenbacks introduced by
Sherman, and Congress did as the bankers demanded with
these notes. Congress issued more than $1,000,000,000, but
we will say or call it $1,000,000,000.

Now let us see what it cost the people; interest and com-
pound interest alone cost the people $1,610,000,000, making
the debt $2,610,000,000 for twenty years, which cost the

bankers only $500,000,000 in Gold. $2,110,000,000 lost or stolen from the people by taking the advice of the bankers. These laws were made for the bankers and against the people by design, and in proof of this I quote John Sherman, "Honest John," Senator of Ohio. When Chairman of the Senate Finance Committee on Dec. 12th, 1867, he said it was found necessary that without the restriction upon the greenbacks the bonds could not be negotiated, and it became necessary to depreciate the notes in order to create a market for the bonds. Bonds! Think of it! Why pay interest on a piece of paper called a bond when we can use another piece of paper and call it greenback and pay no interest at all. Which is the best? For God's sake if we can stand and stick together as a nation on one piece of paper called a bond, because we pay interest on it to Shylocks, we can certainly stick and stand together on the other piece, and pay no interest at all, as both pieces of paper are based on the resources of the American people and the wealth of this great land! The volume of the notes was tripled and the right to convert them taken away under the Act of Feb. 25th, 62-63, which put the exception clause on the back of the currency and made it easy and possible for the bankers to buy $2,610,000,000, gold bearing non-taxable bonds with one half billion dollars ; while the people were robbed of the small amount of $2,110,000,000 by taking the bankers' advice. If that is not true let Sherman and the bankers explain why five hundred and sixty millions dollars is all that it actually cost for the late war. If issued as was the first $60,000,000, no bonds would have been necessary.

(ILLUSTRATION.)

JAN. 1, 1895.	JAN. 1, 1895.
The United States of America promises to pay on demand the sum of $100,000 to bearer, lawful money of the United States.	The United States of America promises to pay the Bank of England the sum of $100,000 in gold coin, with interest at 5 per cent per annum in gold coin of the United States after ten years interest and capital.
(Sd) UNCLE SAM.	(Sd) UNCLE SAM.

There are two papers, both signed by Uncle Sam, the bankers say one is not good ; the other is good because they own the gold, and Uncle Sam has to get some extra gold to

pay the interest on the loan, and for which we send yearly to
England as interest on the bonds and other securities that she
has, the round sum of one hundred and twenty-five millions in
gold, while all the Gold the world produces is only one hundred
and fifty-five millions in gold ; that is the reason why one
paper, the bond, is good, and the other is not.

July 17th, 1861, the law authorizing the issue of treasury
notes was passed; March 17th, 1862, sixty millions dollars of
greenbacks were made full legal tender, no exception clause;
February 25th, 1863, National Banking Law was approved ;
April 12th, 1866, the Funding Act; March 3rd, 1869, Credit
Strengthening Act; July 24th, 1870, Refunding Act; February
12th, 1873, Demonetizing of Silver Act; January 14th, 1875,
Resumption Act ; January 12th, 1888, extended Bank Charter,
and November 1st, 1893, repeal of the Sherman Silver
Purchasing Act. The above laws are the reasons for it, and
they were passed by influence of the bankers ; in evidence, I
quote John Sherman (before he became a Shylock in 1862), he
said in the Senate " I much prefer the credit of the United States, based as it is upon all the productions and properties of the
United States, to the issue of any corporation, however well
guarded and managed."

The monopolizing and "corrupt" newspapers have been
continuously used to fool the people and cover up the wicked
work of the money lenders. Now, readers, please read carefully the following circulars, which were sent out by the
Bankers' Organization on October 9th, 1878, and then make
up your mind what you will do.

AMERICAN BANKERS' ASSOCIATION.

New York, October 9th, 1878.

Dear Sir :

It is advisable to do all in your power to sustain such
prominent daily and weekly newspapers, especially the
Agricultural and Religious Press, as will oppose the issuing
of greenbacks (paper money), and that you also withhold
patronage or favors from all applicants who are not willing to
oppose the Government issue of money. Let the Government
issue the coin and the banks issue the paper money of our

country, for then we can better protect each other, from repealing the law creating National Banks, or restore circulation of Government issue of money, which will be to provide the people with money, and will therefore seriously affect your individual profits as banker and money-lender.

And see your member of Congress at once and engage him to support our interest, that we may control Legislation.

This circular was signed by James Buel, secretary, No. 247 Broadway, New York, and was sent out to nearly all the bankers in the country.

It will be noticed that special effort was to be made to control the Agricultural and Religious Press, and have them oppose the issue of greenbacks; then it says, "See your member of Congress at once," and it is generally believed now that a great many Congressmen were seen and engaged for their work. Two other kinds of circulars were also sent out, one to prominent Republican papers, and the other to prominent Democratic papers; one of them fell into the hands of Colonel Pierce, who was then publishing the Chicago *Inter-Ocean*; Colonel Pierce was a man who believed in fair play, and despised a liar or a coward, and the following is what appeared in the Inter-Ocean after his receipt of the circular.

The *Inter-Ocean* acknowledges the receipt of the following singular document, which came to our office from New York, Saturday morning:

THE AMERICAN BANKERS' ASSOCIATION.
No. 247 Broadway,
Room 4.
New York, Oct. 9th, 1878.

(Strictly private.)
Dear Sir:

Please insert the enclosed printed slip as leaded matter on the Editorial page of your first issue immediately following the receipt of this and send marked copy with bill to

Yours truly,
JAMES BUEL, Secretary,
247 Broadway, Room 4.

Comment on the slip not to exceed half a column ; will be paid for if billed at the same time.   J. B.

The following is the document which we are asked to insert as leaded matter on the Editorial page ; in other words, as statement made by the *Inter-Ocean.*

"The greenback party has offered through its managers to sell out to the Democrats, and hereafter work in Democratic harness, if a place for a few of their leaders can be provided for."

This shows how much dependence there is to be placed on the leaders of the lunatics who clamor for money based on nothing.

We insert this, but we shall send no bill for it ; in the first place we do not follow directions about leading it ; secondly, we can't believe a word of the statement to be true ; the attempt to thus maliciously destroy the Greenback Party without submitting a word of proof, is a piece of brazen effrontery, which ought to be beneath any body of commercial gentlemen, and especially the American Bankers' Association.

Another of the circulars for the Democratic paper fell into the hands of the Editor of the *New York Sun*, another man who refused to accept their bribe. The *Sun* commented as follows, without following instructions : the following circular was received yesterday at the office of the *Sun* :

THE AMERICAN BANKERS' ASSOCIATION.
247 Broadway, New York.

(Strictly private.)

Please insert enclosed slip as Editorial, and send marked copy with bill to

JAMES BUEL, Secretary,
247 Broadway, Room 4.

The prospect is, that in six months there will not be a greenback leader in all the land ; overtures have been made by the leaders of the greenback movement to President Hayes to abandon the greenback as a lost cause, provided he will give good official positions to about twenty of the blatant clamorers for money based on nothing.

You see the presto-change to get the people prejudiced, and also the absurd claim that this great country, with all its resources and all the American people, can only issue money that is based on nothing else but gold.

If we give them all the gold in the world, and then lock them up in one of these islands, and give them nothing for it, the writer would be glad to see them live by looking at it. The writer remembers a case, while in Arizona in 1882 ; two prospectors found a gold nugget, which was so heavy that the two men could not lift it; they both watched it so that no other prospector could come along and claim it; but provisions were getting low, and as no one came to haul the gold away, as they were in the desert, one of the prospectors being more intelligent than the other, said to Jack, "let us bury the gold in the ground, and go after provisions, a mule and tools with which to break it, so that we can go away from here before starving to death." Jack had been cheated once before by a partner in a claim, by taking his partner's advice, and this time he was not going to take any chances. So he said "You can go and try to get more provisions, tools and a mule, and leave me what provisions we have and I will watch the gold;" his partner said, "No, we are too far from a settlement, as we have been three weeks away from the last place we were in, and I take no chances. I take my half of the provisions and go ; you can stay if you want to." So Jack stayed and watched the gold, but it was so far that when his partner came back with the necessaries of life, Jack was dead by the side of the gold.

Now, it will be remembered, that about that time, 1878, the Greenback Party was threatening the annihilation of both the two old rotten parties, and had it not been for the special effort of the bankers, who make their money by loaning money, the Greenback Party would have been victorious long ago.

Those who are familiar with the work of the Reform Movement, can easily detect such articles as the above that are paid for by the money lenders, in most of the great newspapers of the country.

It is high time for the voters to awaken to their own interest, and quit voting for the other fellow. The bankers have no scruples, remember, and will try every device to fool the people.

Readers, please investigate these matters, for it is best that we all understand how our public work is being done, for that, which concerns one, concerns all; if we are being robbed by law, let us find it out. We have made thirty-one thousand millionaires in twenty-five years, and there are about fifty millions of tramps, and they are increasing. In 1866 we had only four millionaires, and they are made by special laws; the baby born to Rothschild inherits one hundred and fifty million of dollars, and it takes more than one hundred thousand men at two dollars per day to pay the interest at five per cent ; it must be paid by labor if paid at all. Astor's income is twenty-five thousand dollars per day, and it takes twenty-five thousand men to pay his income at two dollars per day; allowing one dollar per day for each man to keep himself and his family. This profit must come from labor, and everyone who works helps to pay it.

Think of it, and then see is it not better that the Government issue the money direct to the people on their security, and stop paying interest to Shylocks.

Help to elect people who will carry out the cause of the people.

English bankers send a man over to America to bribe the American House and Senate to demonetize silver.

Ernest Seyd comes over from England with £100,000. A Denver man of high character swears to Seyd's confession, a story of the most gigantic and far-reaching fraud ever perpetrated on the American people.

Mr. Frederick Luckenbach is a citizen of Denver and is well and favorably known by many of Colorado's business men.

STATE OF COLORADO, }
                    } ·SS :
County of Arapahoe. }

FREDERICK LUCKENBACH, being first duly sworn, on oath deposes and says, I am sixty-two years of age ; I was born in Buck County, Pennsylvania; I removed to Philadelphia in the year 1846, and continued to reside there until

1866, when I removed to the city of New York. In
Philadelphia I was in the furniture business; in New York I
branched off into machinery and invention, and I am the
patentee of Luckenbach's Pneumatic Pulverizer, which
machine is now in use in general in the Eastern part of the
United States and Europe. I now reside in Denver, having
removed from New York two years ago. I am well known in
New York; I have been a member of the Produce Exchange,
and I am well acquainted with many members of that body;
I am well-known by Mr. Erastus Wiman. In the year 1865
I visited London, England, for the purpose of placing there
Pennsylvania oil properties, in which I was interested. I
took with me letters of introduction to many gentlemen in
London, among them, one to Mr. Ernest Seyd from Robert
M. Foust, ex-Treasurer of Philadelphia; I became well
acquainted with Mr. Seyd, and with his brother Richard
Seyd, who I understand is yet living. I visited London,
thereafter every year, and at each visit I renewed my
acquaintance with Mr. Seyd, and upon each occasion became
his guest, one or more times joining his family at dinner. In
February, 1874, while on one of those visits, and while his
guest for dinner, I, among other things, alluded to rumors
afloat of Parliamentary corruption, and expressed astonishment that such corruption should exist; in reply to this he
told me he could relate facts about the corruption of the
American Congress that would place it far ahead of the
English Parliament in that line; so far the conversation was
at the dinner table between us; his brother Richard and
others were there also, but this was table talk between Mr.
Ernest Seyd and myself. After the dinner was ended, he
invited me to another room where he resumed the conversation about Legislative corruption; he said "If you will
pledge me your honor as a gentleman not to divulge what I
am about to tell you, while I live, I will convince you that
what I said about the corruption of the American Congress is
true." I gave him the promise, and he continued, "I went
to America in the winter of 1872-3, authorized to secure if I
could the passage of a bill demonetizing silver. It was to the
interest of those I represented, the Governors of the Bank of
England, to have it done; I took with me £100,000.

4

with instructions, that if it was not sufficient to accomplish the object to draw for another £100,000 or as much more as was necessary; he told me that German bankers were interested in having it accomplished; he said he was the financial adviser of the bank. He said, "I saw the Committee of the House and Senate and paid the money and stayed in America until I knew the measure was safe; I asked if he would give me the names of the members to whom he paid the money, but this he declined to do. He said, "*You people will not now comprehend the far-reaching extent of that measure, but will in after years.*" Whatever you may think of corruption in the English Parliament, I assure you I would not have dared to make such an attempt here as I did in your country. I expressed my shame to him for my countrymen in our Legislative bodies. The conversation drifted into other subjects, and after that, though I met him many times, the matter was never again referred to.

(Signed) FREDERICK A.' LUCKENBACH.

Subscribed and sworn to before)
  me at Denver, this Ninth }
  day of May, A. D. 1892.)

(Signed) JAMES A. MILLER,

[SEAL]
Clerk Supreme Court,

State of Colorado.

You will notice the words: "that we would comprehend the importance and far-reaching extent of that law in after years," and I say, readers, that all the American people comprehend it now, if they would only think of it.

Here is another of the Bankers' circulars sent out on March 3rd, 1893, that I copied from an original one, that Grandmaster Workman, J. R. Sovereign of the Knights of Labor, read at a large meeting held at the State Capitol House of Legislature, at Little Rock, Arkansas, where Mr. Sovereign made a brilliant, intelligent and forcible speech for the cause of Labor. Governor W. M. Fishback of said State presided at said meeting.

THE PANIC BULLETIN.

THE AMERICAN BANKERS' ASSOCIATION,

2 WALL STREET AND 90-94 BROADWAY.

NEW YORK, March 3rd, 1893.

To the Bankers of the United States:

DEAR SIR :—The interests of the National Bankers require immediate financial legislation by Congress. Silver, silver certificates and treasury notes should be retired, and national bank notes upon a gold basis made the only money. This will require the authorization of from $500,000,000 to $1,000,000,000 of new bonds as a basis of circulation. You will at once retire one-third of your circulation and call in one-half of your loans. Be careful to make a money stringency felt among your patrons, especially among influential business men. Advocate an extra session of Congress for the repeal of the purchase clause of the Sherman law and act with the other banks of your city in securing a large petition to Congress for its unconditional repeal, per accompanying form. Use personal influence with Congressmen, and particularly let your wishes be known to your Senators. The future life of national banks as fixed and safe investments depends upon immediate action, as there is an increasing sentiment in favor of Government legal tender notes and silver coinage.

EUGENE H. PULLEN, *President.*

The above circular speaks for itself. What the bankers wanted they surely got. When the extra session of Congress was called the purchasing clause of the Sherman law was repealed, and the issue of new bonds to the amount of $262,000,000 secured, with a promise of more coming. As it is planned that after they vote (the chumps) $100,000,000 will be issued, and it is also proposed that if McKinley gets elected, and the plan carried out, $500,000,000 more will be issued. Here is the plan: Senator Sherman, who wrote the gold plank for their platform, is to succeed Carlisle, he will recommend the issue of $500,000,000 of fifty years gold bonds to retire the $500,000,000 paper currency, and issue $445,000,000 National Bank Notes for circulation. Sherman and all the clique newspapers will argue that it will stop the endless chain of depleting his unlawful $100,000,000 gold reserve. At 4 per cent. interest this will give the schemers $1,000,000,000 as interest on the bonds alone, making the debt $1,500,000,000, and if compounded it will be : First year, $520,000,000 ; second year, $540,800,000 ; third year, $562,432,000, and at the end of fifty years it will amount, interest and capital to $3,552,000,000. Think of it ! More than seven times the amount borrowed !! Then the interest on the Bank Notes, too. Oh ! God, please save the American Republic by enlightening the people to see and stop it.

THE AMERICAN BANKERS' ASSOCIATION,

2 WALL STREET AND 90–94 BROADWAY.

NEW YORK, March 23rd, 1896.

To the Bankers of the United States :—At a meeting of the Executive Council of the American Bankers' Association held in this City on March 11th, 1896, the following declaration was made by unanimous vote :

"The Executive Council of the American Bankers' Association declare unequivocally in favor of the maintenance of the existing *gold standard* of value and recommend to all Bankers and of the customers of all banks and exercise of all of their influence as citizens in their various States to select delegates to the political conventions of both the great parties who will declare unequivocally in favor of the *maintenance of the existing gold standard of value.*"

Your influence is earnestly requested to give practical effect to this action.

The next Annual Convention of the Association is to be held in St. Louis, Mo., on September 22nd, 23rd and 24th, 1896, and it is intended to make the Convention of unusual interest to Bankers, and to devote the programme chiefly to the discussion of banking questions by members. To this end short, compact questions involving banking practice or problems are solicited from all parts of the country.

The Association seeks to unite all banks and bankers in one efficient National Organization, and it solicits all National and State Banks, Savings Banks and Banking Firms to become members. For the current year ending September 1st, 1896, the dues are ten dollars for banks with a capital of $100,000 and more, and five dollars for banks having less than $100,000 capital and for private bankers. The advertisement in the Association's Proceedings, sent to all banks and bankers is alone worth the cost of membership. If you desire to join, kindly sign and return enclosed blank.

Special attention is called to the Protective feature of the Association which is developing into great practical benefit. Through it the Association becomes the aggressive agent of its members against professional bank criminals.

Every bank in the United States should co-operate in this important work. The Association recently captured the forgers who swindled a bank in San Francisco out of $20,000 in gold. It has ample evidence to show that criminals know who are members of the Association and are selecting non-members for attack. Ten burglaries yielding over $50,000 were recently committed against non-members, and in one instance a burglary was abandoned because of the discovery that the bank involved was a member of the Association.

JAMES R. BRANCH, *Secretary.*   EUGENE H. PULLEN, *President.*

JOSEPH C. HENDRIX, *Chairman Executive Council.*

The above circular created a sensation in the United States Senate when Senator Butler, of North Carolina read it in the discussion of his bill to stop the issuing of bonds without consent of Congress. Many Senators were taken by surprise, and asked to see it. The bill passed the Senate and went to Congress. Thomas B. Reed was so scared when it was to be reported for final passage that he adjourned Congress, because it would stop the foregoing scheme if passed, and if not, the voters could not be fooled.

MR. CLEVELAND'S COMEDY OF THE BONDS.

Was it ignorance or dishonesty on the part of the Administration when it issued the sixty-two million dollars of bonds of February, 1895, by the private deal of that now famous contract between Carlisle, the Secretary of the Treasury, and the Rothschilds-Morgan-Belmont syndicate, which caused some very sharp pointed and critical articles that were published by the newspapers, irrespective of party affiliation? Mr. Cleveland was wildly attacked for his action in not advertising the sale of said bonds, and thus depriving the people of a chance to bid. The bonds, as a consequence, were sold privately by Mr. Carlisle to his friends, who bought them at their own figures. Was there any good reason for doing this, and wherein was the profit to the people in selling bonds which were worth $120, while the syndicate paid only $104¾? Who was the loser and who got the benefit?

Let us find out the motives. Mr. Cleveland had failed to dictate to the good Democratic Fifty-third Congress his financial ideas as well as a certain plan which did not originate with him, but emanated from his advisers, "the Bankers." These plans consisted since the war in trying to put in the statutes a law giving to the Secretary of the Treasury unlimited power to issue bonds. In this way it would be easier for the bankers to bribe one man, the Secretary, than to fix both houses of Congress.

When Mr. Cleveland saw that there was no more chance or hope for the schemes of his bankers to be successful, and after he had done his best (as his messages show), he got Mr. Carlisle badly scared and rattled. Secretary Carlisle immediately sent for friends to help him. Rothschilds, Belmont, Morgan and Stetson went to Washington and entered into a secret contract with the Secretary of the Treasury for the acquisition of coin bonds, which did not belong to Mr. Carlisle at all, but were the property of the people. Yet, think, that the United States pays good salaries to Mr. Cleveland and Mr. Carlisle to watch for the best interests of the country and the people. The result was that Mr. Carlisle, with Mr. Cleveland's consent, of course, sold to his friends these bonds, the property of the people, at the loss of nearly $10,000,000. This is nothing, however, in comparison with the humiliation imposed upon a country which realizes that it was considered the world over, on account of that transaction, as worthless and resourceless. Will any one deny that Mr. Cleveland and Mr. Carlisle have not violated the moral laws (?) (which are above all artificial laws). No; certainly not, and the Fifty-fourth Congress ought to remind them of their duties. Republicans, Populists and Democrats alike, who are not altogether devoid of the elementary principle of patriotism, who have at heart the cause of *liberty*, and it is the duty of the Senate Committee appointed to investigate the issue and sale of all the bonds to thoroughly investigate this *important* matter, and ask Mr. Cleveland the reason why he should make the people lose such a large amount of money by said queer action, and if no satisfactory reason is given (Mr.Cleveland and Carlisle) ought to be punished for it. This would establish a good precedent, and prevent, in the future, the President and Secretary of the Treasury from violating the laws entrusted to their safe guard.

The conduct of Mr. Cleveland as a President is worthy to be compared with the magnificent promises of fidelity and honesty made by him when he said : " *Public office is a Public Trust; Office Holders are the Servants of the People—not their Masters.*" And also in his first inaugural address as President in 1884. Here are his words :

"FELLOW CITIZENS :—In the presence of this vast assemblage of my country-men I am about to supplement, and seal by the oath which I shall take, the mani-festation of the will of a great and free people. In the exercise of their power, and the right of self-government, they have committed to one of their fellow-citizens a supreme and sacred trust, and he here consecrates himself to their service. This impressive ceremony adds little to the solemn sense of responsibility with which I contemplate the duty I owe to all the people of the land. Nothing can relieve me from anxiety, *lest by any act of mine their interests may suffer*, and nothing is needed to strengthen my resolution to engage every faculty and effort in the promotion of their welfare."

Such are the very words pronounced by Mr. Cleveland, and I have already shown how he acted wrongly in the matter of bonds.

To make the facts more plain, let us make an illustration of fact. Suppose that a wholesale grocery firm has an agency in charge of a trusted employee. For some cause the firm is compelled to sell its goods at short notice so as to obtain ready cash money. This is not the case, by the way, with the Government of the United States, which has the right to " coin " (make) money without selling any bonds. But for the sake of argument we proceed. If the employee at the agency, who is supposed to be familiar with the business methods, is honest, if he studies the interest of his employer, he will advertise extensively what he has to sell, so as to get the people to bid on and obtain the highest possible prices for the goods. Now, if instead of doing this, he disposes of the goods *privately*, under hand, and at a ridiculous figure in favor of his friends, will the firm keep him in its employ? Common sense says no. Indeed it is more than certain that the firm will discharge him, if not make him materially responsible for his dishonest transaction, and have him punished, *unless the firm is composed of a pack of fools*. In the matter of this $62,000,000 of bonds, this is exactly what Mr. Cleveland has done. He has effected the sale of the bonds without advertising, for fear of bidders, so as to give undue advantage to his friends, the Bankers. It was claimed and denied that a similar sale had been planned for the last $100,000,000 bonds. But the indignation and pressure of the press and the people, changed the plan, if there was one, and Carlisle advertised for bids for it, and these last bonds brought nearly three times as much premiums as the previous ones, which were longer bonds, and really worth more.

WHY THE BONDS WERE NOT ADVERTISED.

The writer will explain why Cleveland and Carlisle sold the bonds to their friends. These bonds will become matured in thirty years, bearing interest at $3\frac{3}{4}$ per centum per annum. This will give to the syndicate who bought these bonds over $2,000,-000 per annum for interest alone, beside the large bonus of 90 per cent., according to the National Banking Law, which I have showed. By adding this 90 per cent, which the law gives them, when a deposit of said bonds is made with the Secretary of the Treasury, they became worth $117,800,000. For this reason the bankers make their deposit as soon as they receive the bonds. Mr. Cleveland, in his message of January 28, 1895, wanted Congress to increase this bonus from 90 per cent. to 100 per cent., so as to make his friends worth not only the $62,000,000, plus 90 per cent., but double the original amount, or $124,000,000, for the term of thirty years. A good scheme, was it not?

HOW YOU ARE ROBBED.

TO UNCLE SAM.

You had better watch for the future raids of those fellows, because they intend to put you on a gold standard, and you will never get out of debt to them.

ARE THE BONDS VALID?

The answer is emphatically NO, a thousand times no! and this is as plain as daylight. The contract entered into by Carlisle and the syndicate of bankers is, in itself, a pure piece of effrontery. For instance, one of the clauses of this contract reads thus:

"Should the Secretary of the Treasury desire to offer or sell bonds of the United States on or before October 1st, 1895, he shall offer the same to the parties of the second part (the syndicate); but thereafter he shall be free from such obligation to the parties of the second part."

Such a privilege was never sold or granted to any one. If the United States should have been involved in a war, the country would have been thrown into a regular state of financial anarchy, as it just happened later during the Venezuela imbroglio. By the above clause the outsiders were practically shut out; it is probably for this reason alone that the syndicate agreed to another Jesuitic promise in the following terms:

"* * * The parties of the second part (the syndicate), as far as lies in their power, will exert all financial influences, and will make all legitimate efforts to protect the Treasury of the United States against the withdrawals of gold pending the complete performance of this contract."

This kind of protection is more than amazing. Think of these virtuous (?) and disinterested bankers protecting the United States Treasury against the assaults of Wall Street. Truly Mr. Cleveland and Carlisle are great financiers in their way; they remind one of the man who engaged the wolf as a shepherd to guard his sheep and intrusted his chickens to the good care of Maitre Reinard (the fox).

When the United States, the richest country in the world, has come to the point that its credit can be kept up only by men such as Rothschilds, Belmont and Morgan, the American people had better remain silent and boast no more of their great wealth and patriotism. Our credit is good, however, with or without the gambling scheme established by Sherman, and providing for an unlawful $100,000,000 gold reserve. Was there any such reserve in 1863, 1864, 1865 and 1866? No; the country was good enough to support its credit. The administration went back to Statutes of 1862, when the country was involved in a

civil war, to find authority for its acts. Section 3,700 of the
Revised Statutes, which establishes this issue of bonds, reads as
follows :

"That the Secretary of the Treasury may purchase coin with any of the bonds
or notes of the United States, authorized at such rates and upon such terms as he
may deem most advantageous to the public interest."

Did the Secretary of the Treasury think the rates he obtained
were the most advantageous for public interest, and did he ask
if any one else wanted to offer more?   Certainly not !

This is not all, however, as the law invoked by Mr. Cleveland had been practically repealed in 1866, as the document
printed below will sufficiently prove :

In the Senate April 9th, 1866.

WAYS AND MEANS COMMITTEE.

Mr. Fessenden (Senator from Maine)—I move that the Senate proceeds to the
consideration of the bill (II. R. No. 207) to amend "An act to provide ways and
means to support the Government," approved March 3d, 1865.

The motion was agreed to, and the bill was considered as in Committee of the
Whole.   It is proposed by this measure to enact that the act entitled "An act to
provide ways and means to support the Government," approved March 3d, 1865,
shall be extended and construed to authorize the Secretary of the Treasury, at his
discretion, to receive any treasurey notes or other obligations issued under any act
of Congress, whether bearing interest or not, in exchange for any description of
bonds authorized by the act to which this is an amendment, and also to dispose of
bonds authorized by that act, either in the United States or elsewhere, to such an
amount, in such manner, and at such rates as he may think advisable for lawful
money of the United States, or for any treasury notes, certificates of indebtedness,
or other representatives of value, which have been or which may be issued under
any act of Congress, the proceeds thereof to be used only for retiring treasury notes
or other obligations issued under any act of Congress ; *but it is not to be construed to
authorize any increase in the public debt.*"

"When the last sentence to the Act was read," said the Congressional records, "Mr. Sherman, of Ohio, actually jumped to
his feet."   And no wonder ! as this law was the inauguration of
a policy intended to put a stop to the increase of the public
debt, thwarting at the same time the gambling schemes of
Honest John, who has kept up the fight without interruption
ever since.

The bill passed, nevertheless, with the following votes :

YEAS—Messrs. Antony, Brown, Buckalew, Clark, Conness, Cowan, Cragin,
Davis, Doolittle, Edmunds, Fessenden, Foster, Grimes, Guthrie, Harris, Johnson,
Kirkwood, Lane, of Indiana ; McDougall, Morgan, Morrill, Nesmith, Nye, Poland,
Pomeroy, Riddle, Sumner, Trumbull, Vanwinkle, Willey, Williams and Wilson

NAYS—Messrs. Chandler, Howard, Howe, Morton, Ramsey, Sherman and Wade—7.

ABSENT—Messrs. Creswell, Dixon, Henderson, Hendricks, Stewart, Wright and Yates.

Furthermore, the records concerning the final passage of the bill amending the Act, reads thus :

HOUSE OF REPRESENTATIVES,

April 10th, 1866.

Message from the Senate by Mr. Forney, its Secretary, announced that the Senate had passed a joint resolution and bills (among which was this one) of the following title, in which the concurrence of the House was requested : An act (H. R., 207) to amend an act entitled "An act to provide ways and means to support the Government," March 3d, 1865.

ENROLLED BILL SIGNED.

Mr. Trowbridge, from the Committee on Enrolled Bills, reported that the Committee had examined and found truly enrolled a bill (H. R., 207) entitled, etc., etc. Whereupon the Speaker signed the same.

HOUSE OF REPRESENTATIVES,

Friday, April 13th, 1866.

MESSAGE FROM THE PRESIDENT.—A message in writing was received from the President of the United States by Mr. William G. Moore, his Secretary ; also informing the House that he had approved and signed bills and resolutions of the following titles, namely : An act (H. R. No. 207) to amend an act to provide ways and means to support the Government, approved March 3d, 1865.

Is it possible (?) that Mr. Cleveland or Mr. Carlisle were ignorant of the bill and law which condemns positively their present financial actions and schemes ? It cannot be possible. As to John Sherman, he does not want to remember, and this book is written to refresh his memory.

There is no question or doubt that the public debt has been increased $200,000,000, and that the money received from said bonds has been used to incur the current expenses of the govern. ment, which it must provide for its support by tariff or tax and not by bonding the country and the people forever to a Gold Bugs' ring. The writer has not found any repeal of this law, and it will be better for the people to not invest in any such bonds. In the discussion in the United States Senate of the Butler Bond Resolution, Mr. Brown, Senator from Utah ; Quay, of Pennsylvania ; Allen, of Nebraska, and several others, said that the bonds were invalid, and may be repudiated at maturity.

PANIC OF 1893.

The readers certainly remember the panic of 1893, precipitated upon the country by the President, in pursuance of the bankers' purpose to strike the final blow at silver in order to complete their work by compelling the repeal of the purchasing clause of the Sherman Act. What was the pretext upon which that repeal was strenuously demanded and fiercely enforced (by patronage)? It was said that the purchases of silver had the effect to drive gold from the country, was this true? No; it was either a delusion or a wilful misrepresentation. After a prolonged struggle, during which foolish men even talked as if the Senate of the United States had no right to oppose itself to the will of the President (and there are yet such people that criticize the Senate for wanting to remonetize silver), but should accept the President's command with unquestioning obedience, the repeal was accomplished. Now note the result. Here are some figures taken from the report of the Bureau of Statistics of the Treasury Department, and, therefore, indisputably authentic (pages 307 and 308 report for September, 1894).

GOLD EXPORTS BEFORE AND AFTER REPEAL OF THE PURCHASE ACT.

	1893.	1894.
Gross exports nine months to September 30	$76,278,514	$90,506,508
Net exports nine months to September 30	10,317,882	73,815,163

Here we have proof that during the first nine months of 1894, after repeal of the silver purchase clause, gold left the country more than seven times faster than it did in the corresponding period in the previous year, before the repeal of the clause. And to-day, nearly three years after President Cleveland succeeded in accomplishing his purpose, the condition of the treasury, with respect to gold, is far worse than it was when he created the uproar.

The gold bug press, the bankers and the Republican party supporters are again busily telling the country that a return to bimetalism would bring ruin. Those same fellows said that after the repeal of the Sherman Act (which put $4,000,000 monthly in circulation), good times and prosperity would return.

Did it return? No; and they now try to tell the same old story. Will we believe it? They speak so much of sound money, yet themselves ignore what sound money is, growling that we must have sound money which does not depreciate, and they claim gold as the only money which will not depreciate. Will they oblige the people by explaining what was the matter with the fifty million dollars of Treasury notes issued July 17th, 1861, which Congress on March 17th, 1862, made a full legal tender? Were not these notes worth 5 per cent. more than gold as soon as they were made full legal tender? Yes! This is a fact to remind them that if gold is demonetized it will fall in value.

What the writer believes honest, sound money, is that kind of money which is issued by the government in good faith, which the people will accept without discount for labor and properties, such as they have to sell or exchange. Such money is issued by the government to the people on their security without having the bankers to monopolize it like they do with gold. Now the bankers will lend any one gold on their notes, secured by a first mortgage on their property, which furnishes the necessaries of life. Gold, on the contrary, is only a commodity, as there is more intrinsic value in a bushel of wheat than all the gold in existence in the world, when one comes to facts. Is it possible to eat gold? They say, also, that the greenbacks issued during the war were so depreciated that they fell to about 40 or 50 cents on the dollar, and for this reason they say we should not have greenbacks or 50-cent-dollars. The money sharks will not divulge that it was after Mr. Lincoln's example of starting the coining of money (legal tenders), backed by the whole people producing the necessaries of life,—wheat, corn, pork, beef, cotton, etc.,—which Europe, especially England, must have, under the penalty of starving, they saw that they could not have the monopoly of the currency that was going to take the place of cowardly gold, which would surely depreciate; it was then they planned the gold conspiracy.

The right to issue money (the life blood of nations) under the Constitution is vested in Congress, and the Supreme Court affirms it, but Congress has transferred this great power to National Banks, authorizing them to issue bank notes, and the people do take said notes in good faith, giving their honest goods or labor for it ! but when the people have to pay to the government some duties on their imports, the goverment tells them that the notes are no good and that they have to get gold to pay the duties and get their imports. Why is it that the government gives to the bankers authority to issue bank notes when the government refuses to take them ?

Now, suppose, I would give authority to my agent to issue a note to you for $100, promising to pay you the same, and get your goods. You take it in good faith, and you do not look on the back of the note and see the exception clause I put on it, which reads, without recourse to me.

In the course of a month or so it happens that you have to pay me some dues, rent, etc., and you bring the note that my agent gave you to pay it with, and then I say to you that the note is not good, and tell you that you have to get gold to pay me the dues. What would you say ? Would you say that I acted honestly ? No ; you would say, " Why did you allow the issuing and giving of a note to me which you knew was no good, and that you would not take back ? " And for good reasons you could call me a defrauder and swindler and obtainer of goods on false pretences.

This is exactly the case of the United States Government and the National Bank notes which the people take in good faith and deliver their honest goods for, without reading the swindling and dishonest clause on the back of it. Read it when you get one, and then you will say that the policy of the Government is beyond a doubt dishonest on its part in giving the National Bankers authority to issue Bank Notes, when the Government which gives the authority refuses to accept the notes for duties on imports and interest on debts, and if some one sounds the alarm he is called a crank. There have been many cranks in this world, such as Columbus, Morse and many others. So far it takes cranks to make the world move, and the crank for that matter must be strongly applied to the financial wheel of our country, or before long the finances will be ground to pieces, and they may think then that the crank is a dangerous thing to fool with.

LOOTING THE TREASURY.

First Raid.

A statement of the cash in the United States Treasury is issued every thirty days by the Secretary of the Treasury, John G. Carlisle. This document is public property. Write or ask for one, and you get it, for any month you name. The following statistical facts are copied from these reports:

CASH IN THE UNITED STATES TREASURY FOR DECEMBER, 1893.

"Gold coin and bars, one hundred and fifty-eight million, three hundred and three thousand, seven hundred and seventy-seven dollars and thirteen cents. Silver coins and silver bars, five hundred million, three hundred and ten thousand, five hundred twenty-eight dollars and seventy-six cents. Greenbacks, gold, coin and silver certificates and bank notes, sixty-two million, eight hundred and forty six thousand, one hundred and fifty-eight dollars and sixty-six cents. Other forms counted as money, fifteen million, one hundred and fifty-four thousand, one hundred and thirty-four dollars and forty-eight cents. Total, $736,614,599.03."

With the above vast amount of money in the treasury, the next month, February, 1894, Grover Cleveland, without law, or any authority, or any need, except that which is and always has been exercised by tyrants—usurpation—ordered John G. Carlisle to design, engrave, stamp and print fifty million dollars of untaxed United States bonds, with an interest charge of twenty million dollars. There are two classes of our people who endorse this proceeding, first, the officials to the deal, bankers, money loaners, millionaires, pawn shops and plunderers of the people, and second, FOOLS, those persons who are fools for the want of ordinary, common sense on financial questions !

Second Raid.

CASH IN THE TREASURY, OCTOBER, 1894.

"Gold coin and bars, one hundred and twenty-five million, six hundred and thirteen thousand, eight hundred and ninety-five dollars and seventy-three cents. Silver coins and bars, five hundred and six million, eighteen thousand, seven hundred and fourteen dollars and seventy-four cents. Greenbacks, gold, coin and silver certificates and bank notes, one hundred and six million, five hundred and seven thousand, one hundred and fifty-four dollars and forty cents. Making a grand total of $738,139,564.87.

With the vaults bursting with the above-named grades of money, Grover Cleveland, for the second time, without law or authority, ordered the next month, November, 1894, Carlisle to print and sell to the Stewart Syndicate, fifty million dollars, United States bonds, running thirty years, with an interest charge of over sixty million dollars.

Endorsers of this stupendous steal—first, the whining sycophants in official life, the thirteen New York banks that got the bonds, at a cost of a little more than ten cents on the dollar, and leading daily papers owned by the bankers and bond buyers, and second, the American peasantry who vote the Democratic or Republican ticket because dad did so, and will not think for themselves.

Third Raid.

CASH IN THE TREASURY, DECEMBER, 1894.

"Gold coin and bars, one hundred and thirty-nine million, six hundred and six thousand, three hundred and fifty-four dollars and five cents. Silver coins and bars, five hundred and four millions, forty-five thousand, four hundred and fifty-six dollars and forty cents. Greenbacks, gold, coin and silver certificates and bank notes, one hundred and twenty-two million, nine hundred and fourteen thousand, seven hundred and fifty-nine dollars and seventy-two cents. Other forms, used as money, sixteen million, one hundred and ninety-seven thousand, seven hundred and nineteen dollars and forty-three cents. Grand total. $782,764,289.60."

With this incomprehensible sum of money in the possession of Carlisle, Grover Cleveland and his secretary invites the most infamous Tories on American soil, the agents of Nathan Rothschilds & Co., from Wall Street, and, after being closeted with these brigands for three days, in the White House, in rooms and halls consecrated by the precious foot-prints of our illustrious dead, and after this secret counsel, boldly, brutishly and defiantly informed the American people, through a lot of venal, lunkheads in Congress that he had sold $62,400,000 untaxed bonds, running thirty years, at 104 on the dollar, when their market price that day was 120. Net profit on the deal was $9,984,000. Proof is overwhelming and conclusive that this amount was divided between the clique and their associates. Amount of interest to be collected on this deal will foot up about eight million dollars. As these English Tories wave their victorious red flag and flaunt their red suits under God's beautiful sunlight, the American patriot falls on his knees, weeping and praying, as he hears this British octopus, crushing the bones of that gallant band, the Grand Army of the Republic and their children, and into this charnal sepulcher of horrors hurling with relentless fury the poor old bones of the Confederate soldier, his widows and orphan children.

Fourth Raid.

CASH IN THE TREASURY, DECEMBER, 1895.

"The December report of Carlisle shows $787,678,447.62 in the Treasury, of which $113,198,707.97 was gold coin and bars, and $157,567,096.78 was in paper money, the greater part of the latter being greenbacks.

While patriots slept, the looters plotted, and at the dead hour of midnight, in January, 1896, the announcement was flashed over the wires that $100,000,000 of untaxed bonds had been tied on the necks of the great American peasantry, with an interest charge of four million dollars per year for the next thirty years. Men who will submit to such outrages are no longer free men, but SLAVES.

With such a large amount of money in the treasury and not knowing what to do with it, yet the administration goes on and issues bonds to obtain more money. This method of financiering reminds one of a farmer who had his farm clear of mortgages and plenty of money in his safe, which he had no place to invest or use, yet for the sake of obtaining more money, mortgaged his farm and then locked it up, with the other money, for the purpose of keeping up his credit, which (in the first place), was good. The interest on the mortgage finally swallowed up his farm. Now this is exactly what the present administration has done.

The bonds are obtained with the people's money, to wit: The Secretary has authority, under the National Banking Laws, to designate any National Bank as a U. S. depository, and he deposits with said banks treasury notes and greenbacks. When the scheme is to be worked, the favorite banks will prance on the subtreasury in New York and withdraw gold for these notes and lower the gold reserve. Then the cry, "Your credit is running down" is started. "Issue bonds." They are issued, and our gold is paid in again. The bankers draw 90 per cent. in greenbacks and, by adding 10 per cent., he is able to pay back the amount of original deposit made by the Secretary, until another raid is planned so that the bankers can get more bonds.

5

CLEVELAND'S SPECIAL MESSAGE OF JAN. 28, 1895.

He is not satisfied with regular messages to carry out the bankers' plans and shoots in special ones. This one sounds like and corroborates the (panic bulletin) bankers' secret circulars of March 3d, 1893. I wonder if it originated from the same source? All the bankers in the country liked the message. See what the President of the American Bankers' Association said about it.

" With natural resources unlimited in variety and productive strength, and with a people whose activity and enterprise seek only a fair opportunity to achieve national success and greatness, our progress should not be checked by a financial policy and a heedless disregard of sound monetary laws, nor should the timidity and fear which they engender stand in the way of our prosperity.

The real trouble which confronts us consists in a lack of confidence, widespread, and constantly increasing, in the continuing ability or disposition of the Government to pay its obligations in gold. This lack of confidence grows to some extent out of the palpable and apparent embarrassment attending the efforts of the Government under existing laws to procure gold, and to a greater extent out of the impossibility of either keeping it in the Treasury or cancelling obligations by its expenditure after it is obtained. "

Do not be scared Mr. President, our credit is good, the resources are here and are ours (you stated) and why should we give them away to Shylocks as interest on bonds. Please see section (8) article (5) of our constitution, which says Congress shall have power to coin money and regulate the value thereof.

Mr. President if you do not know what you are doing or talking about, you had better give up the job, and do not try to tell 65,000,000 people that bonds, mortgages, or interest paying debts are good things to have. Yes, they may be for the bankers, but how about the people?

The only way left open to the Government for procuring gold is by the issue and sale of United States bonds. The only bonds that can be so issued were authorized nearly twenty-five years, and are not well calculated to meet our present needs. Among other disadvantages they are made payable in coin instead of specifically in gold.

Conditions are certainly supervening tending to make the bonds which may be issued to replenish our gold less useful for that purpose.

An adequate gold reserve is in all circumstances absolutely essential to the upholding of our public credit and to the maintenance of our high national character.

Our gold reserve has again reached such a stage of diminution as to require its speedy reinforcement.

The aggravations that must inevitably follow present conditions and methods will certainly lead to misfortune and loss, not only to our national credit and prosperity and to financial enterprise, but to those of our people who seek employment as a means of livelihood and to those whose only capital is their daily labor.

I suggest that the bonds be issued in denominations of twenty and fifty dollars and their multiples, and that they bear interest at a rate not exceeding three per cent per annum. I do not see why they should not be payable fifty years from their date. We of the present generation have large amounts to pay if we meet our obligations, and long bonds are most salable. The Secretary of the Treasury might well be permitted, at his discretion, to receive on the sale of bonds the legal tender and Treasury notes to be retired, and, of course, when they are thus retired or redeemable in gold they should be cancelled.

These bonds, under existing laws, could be deposited by national banks as security for circulation ; and such banks should be allowed to issue circula tion up to the face value of these or any other bonds so deposited.

As a constant means for the maintenance of a reasonable supply of gold in the Treasury, our duties on imports should be paid in gold, allowing all other dues to the Government to be paid in any other form of money.

Mr. Cleveland is heart and soul for all the schemes and traps of the Bankers, and John Sherman, to give the Bankers a right to rob the people in a country of equal right (?) to all and privilege to none.

BANKERS LIKE THE MESSAGE.

The message is sound and straightforward. Its suggestions are in accord with the *Herald's* popular loan proposition and meet my ideas exactly. If the suggestions are carried out by Congress the remedy for financial ills is at hand.

This is what Mr. E. H. Pullen (chairman) of the American Bankers' Association said about the message : Mr. Pullen is the gentleman that denied and said that the circular sent out by the American Bankers' Association to all the Bankers on March 3d, 1893, the one that Mr. R. J. Sovereign read at Little Rock, Arkansas, was a lie made of whole cloth (was it ?)

I indorsed the popular loan plan from the moment the *Herald*, proposed it and still insist that it is the practical solution of the financial problem. — President Simmons, Fourth National Bank.

I approve every word of President Cleveland's message. He has taken the right stand in the matter, and shows how imperative is the need of the popular loan, as advised long ago by the *Herald*. — Cashier Leech, National Union Bank.

Double leaded editorials, N. Y. *Herald*, Jan. 29th, 1895.

McKINLEY ENDORSES CLEVELAND.

In answer to the Nomination Notification Committee, Mr. McKinley, the Republican nominee for President, endorses Cleveland for having issued bonds in time of peace. Certainly he endorses Cleveland. Why not? Cleveland is a Mugwump and adopted the Republican financial policy. There is no differ. ence on this policy between Cleveland and John Sherman. They agree in enriching themselves and their friends at the expense of the people. Sherman said in the Senate that there was not the least doubt about how Mr. McKinley stood on the money question. That he, as a Republican, was pledged to the Republican policy (that of contracting the currency), and Sherman also had the courage to say in open debate in the Senate that he would rather take the *last shirt from the backs of the people* in order to pursue the Republican policy of keeping up the credit of the country. I wonder if Sherman would give his last shirt to the bankers? He was a poor man, but now he is a multi-millionaire. How did he make it? Grover Cleveland at the age of seventeen worked for $4 a week for Rodgers, Bowen & Rodgers in Buffalo, N. Y., and wanted to go West. Then the very West and South, which he antagonizes and calls wild, produced the greater part of the wealth that has been wrongly appropriated for the enrichment of the few. He, too, is now a multi-millionaire. How did he get it?

McKinley is poor and a little popular, and the Bankers pick him up to use him. Hanna has spent $150,000, and will spend more. Why? The readers can guess that for themselves. Here is what the Philadelphia *Item*, a silver Republican paper, says editorially, on July 2, 1896 :

NOW THE PEOPLE KNOW WHAT TO EXPECT.

" To the formal notice announcing the choice of the National Republican Convention, Mr. McKinley replied : 'The complaint of the people is not against the Administration for borrowing money and issuing bonds to preserve the credit of the country, but against the ruinous policy which made this necessary.'

" That remark at once puts Mr. McKinley in the boots of President Cleveland, so far as the endless chain business of more bond issues for gold is concerned.

" It is an open declaration that when the time comes, he, like President Cleveland, will issue bonds to get gold 'to preserve the credit of the country.'

" For, he says, that has never been the complaint of the people.

" What rank nonsense !

" So here the public has it in plain language. Mr. McKinley, if he gets the chance, proposes to continue the very tactics of President Cleveland to make this country poorer by an additional bonded indebtedness in times of peace.

"*The Item* informs Mr. McKinley that there has not existed under the present Administration any 'ruinous policy' which has made the recent bond issues necessary. If Congress spent more money than its appropriations called for, it was not the business of the President to issue bonds therefor. And whatever 'ruinous policy' there is in the Administration adhering to an exclusive gold standard, is all of its own unlawful and unnecessary making."

THE BANKERS MEAN WHAT THEY SAY.

The public must, in self-defense, do their own banking.

In conformity with "The Item's" recent editorials, explaining how the money lenders are urging panic measures to intimidate borrowers and the public to vote for a gold monometalic ticket, is the general press dispatch that the banks of Louisville, Ky., have already taken a bold stand, by a mutual agreement, "to refuse to lend any money to any man who favors free silver. It makes no difference who he is, he cannot get a cent at any Louisville bank on any terms or security."

"Several Louisville banks sent for some of their pronounced silver patrons, and requested them to withdraw their accounts. There was no other reason given for this conduct than the statement: 'You are trying to destroy our business, therefore, we protect ourselves. We desire no further business with you.'"

This may prove staggering information for a good many honest people in this city, who, heretofore, have looked upon the managers of influential banks as above reproach in honor and integrity.

"*The Item*" is very much mistaken in estimation of the American character, if it turns out that this form of intimidation does not raise a revolt in the public mind that will teach these money lenders a lesson they will not quickly forget.

There was a law recently passed at Washington, making it a crime for sundry corporations to unite in "restraint of trade."

If the conduct of these Louisville bankers is not a "restraint of trade" of the largest dimensions, it is not known here what to call it.

That our government should put the exclusive control of all money loaned to trade and industry in the hands of, as is here shown, unscrupulous people, who do not hesitate to use it to intimidate our people into voting for more profits to money lenders, is monstrous enough in itself ; but when it is remembered that this same power was used in 1893, and is now threatening again to extend its influence in the same way over the entire country, it at once becomes a crime of the first magnitude.

This government acts the part of a fool which puts its entire resources of loans of money exclusively in the hands of those who use it to oppress its people. There is not the slightest need or excuse for it, whatever.

From the *Memphis Evening Star* (Rep.) May 8, 1894.

The Devil's favorite combination : Wall Street, John Sherman and Grover Cleveland   *   *   *

John Sherman will never be happy until the Government orders another bond issue, says the *Arkansas Gazette*, and then he and Cleveland will be in a condition to repose side by side on the same downy couch, the wolf and the leech, so to speak, will be room-mates.

OUR COUNTRY'S DEFECTIVE POLICY.

Our present National Banking System was established by the Government, presumably for the benefit of the people. We have seen the favored institution, after being nurtured to life, fix their poisonous fangs into the breast of their common mother, and attempt to destroy her life. With the proverbial weakness of a mother, the United States has borne her wrong in silence. She has forgiven the ingratitude of her children, and has drawn them closer to her lacerated bosom. But our country has other children besides these favored vipers, and they are injured by her unreasonable tenderness and partiality. Yet those other children in their affection for the mother have silently endured their unjust treatment. They have seen that portion of her children who contribute nothing to her support inflict burdensome debts upon those who toil, and who alone have supported her, and supplied her chest with millions which were appropriated for the benefit of the ungrateful Bankers, who want everything to the detriment of others.

That the present banking system is defective is demonstrated by the panics instituted which have cost the country in round numbers, to wit, $228,000,000 in 1873, averaging about $200,-000,000 a year for six years during the adjustment to the specie basis; then again below $100,000,000. In 1883, $226,000,000, dropping to $124,000,000 the next year. Finally in 1893 the loss amounted to $550,000,000, making a grand total of $2,628,000,000 in all, and not accounting for the loss for the period between the years 1885 to 1892 inclusive, which were enormous. The only remedy to the situation consists in the Government establishing banks of its own on the post office plan, and the Government to be the only authority to issue money (according to the Constitution, which has been violated by a Republican Congress in transferring this great power to issue money to National Banks, which the Constitution itself forbids, and does not say that Congress may transfer said power). The Government cannot fail, on account of its own resources, and therefore panics could not be possible. The people would borrow from the people, and this would lessen the rate of interest. Should a high rate of interest become necessary the amount paid would return to the people.

A DEFECTIVE BANKING SYSTEM.

Admitted by the Bankers themselves in their Convention at Chicago in 1885. To prove that the present National Banking System is defective, I will conclusively show by the statement and testimony of the Bankers themselves, and therefore submit to the readers herewith the following table and figures compiled by W. W. Flannagan, Cashier of the Commercial National Bank of New York. It was submitted by Mr. Flannagan to the Convention of the American Bankers' Association, which was held at Chicago, September 23rd and 24th, 1885, and was adopted and ordered printed with the proceedings of the convention. It is now preserved at the Boston New Public Library. It is entitled, " Security for National Bank Depositors."

PEOPLE'S LOSS ON ACCOUNT OF NATIONAL BANK FAILURES.

Compiled by W. W. Flannagan, Cashier of the Commercial National Bank of New York, therefore cannot be disputed, because they were adopted at the Bankers' Convention.

YEARS OF FAILURES.	PROVED CLAIMS AGAINST INSOLVENT NATIONAL BANKS.	CLAIMS REMAINING UNPAID OR DEPOSITORS' LOSS.
1865	$122,809	$51,277
1866	1,163,699	871,192
1867	3,358,103	889,991
1868	307,804	82,787
1869	239,836	53,125
1870	....	....
1871	2,463,704	....
1872	515,648	124,587
1873	6,677,712	1,587,201
1874	331,997	144,753
1875	2,366,818	1,725,135
1876	1,332,410	365,384
1877	4,745,541	857,825
1878	2,010,294	352,773
1879	465,685	32,799
1880	778,966	1,081,314
1881	2,703,285	2,633,230
1882	3,148,022	....
1883	522,332	....
1884	5,285,815	....
Total	38,479,810	Total 14,776,659

"Twenty-five years ago," *said Mr. Flannagan in the first paragraph,* "if it had been proposed in the abstract to organize a systhem of banking whereby the circulating notes of banks, no matter where issued, should pass at par from Maine to Florida, and that not only the notes of solvent banks should pass current, but the notes of insolvent banks as well, the most experienced and wisest banker, under the system then in vogue, would have pronounced it *impossible.*

"Familiar as we are with the National Banking System, which has gradually developed this result, there appears to us nothing strange in this state of facts, and we only wonder that we endured the evils of the prior system for more than fifty years. Under the State System (with the exception of New York, Louisiana and Massachusetts), we had no real security for circulation, and to keep the issues of the banks afloat seemed to be the difficulty of the managers of that day, they experienced no difficulty in the payment of their depositors as long as provision was made for their circulation, for, with the latter, either directly or indirectly, they managed to prevent the former feeling any uneasiness. Bank failures came from inability to redeem circulation—not from inability to pay depositors. Now, under the National Banking System, failures never come from inability to redeem circulating notes, but exclusively from inability to pay depositors.

"To-day the practical question arises : Can we not take another step forward in the improvement of the National Banking System, whereby the same confidence which now exists in the mind of the holder of a note, shall also exist in the mind of a depositor, and that virtually the one shall be equally secured with the other. This being done, we shall have no more runs on National Banks, no more wild panics by reason of the fear of loss therefrom, no Clearing House loan certificates, no needless failures."

Here we have the conclusive proof and facts showing that the present banking system is defective, and that the depositors must take the chances on receiving back their deposits, because the banker can fail when he wants to, and makes money out of such failure. Mr. Flannagan, in continuation, wanted the repeal of the tax on National Bank circulation as the only remedy and solution of the defect, which, of course, was accepted and adopted by his associate bankers in the convention. The writer would like to ask Mr. Flannagan, or any other National Banker, how the repeal of the tax on National Bank circulation would stop and cure the mismanagement and frauds committed by dishonest Bankers? Let them come to the front and prove how the repeal of the tax would stop the wild speculations and gambling on stock exchanges and race horses, real estate deals, etc., with the depositor's money. No! dishonesty will continue until the Government establishes banks of its own, and honesty takes care of the people's money.

Why did the money lenders of the world want to get hold of American resources? They looked for a fresh, new field and found in the United States a bonanza. Europe was heavily mortgaged and they did not care to lend much more money there. This is the reason why American bonds are preferred and in great demand. The following figures may be of interest:

"If the richness of a country should be measured by the amount of its national debt, Europe must be immensely wealthy. The following may prove interesting in this respect. The figures represent francs, the value of which is based on the twenty-franc gold-piece : England owes 41,500,000,000 ; France, 30,481,158,926 ; Austria, 15,875,611,153.20 centimes ; Germany, 14,366,955,667.50 centimes ; Italy, 11,000,-000,000 ; Spain, 5,000,000,000, of which 1,342,640 are due to government employes ; Turkey, 2,600,000,000 ; Belgium, 2,000,000,000 ; Roumania, 1,000,-000,000 ; Greece, 730,979,175 ; Portugal, 668,205,869 ; Sweden and Norway, 582,677,236.78 centimes : Servia, 340,692,542 ; Denmark, 227,661,982 ; Switzerland, 64,546,821 ; Luxemburg, 16,500,000 ; Montenegro, 2,500,000. Neglecting smaller countries, which are also largely indebted, this makes a grand total of 126,000,000,000, which bear at 4 per cent. an interest amounting to 4,040,000,000 francs yearly. The taxpayers have to foot the bill, as a matter of course."

THE ENLARGEMENT OF DEBT OF OUR COUNTRY BY FALLING PRICES.

But there is another and more serious consequence of the persistent decline of prices, a consequence to which the friends of the British gold-standard are quite averse to alluding in their discussions of the subject. As prices go down the dimensions of all fixed obligations experience enlargement. The whole world is in debt. In our own country, in 1890, the State, national, city and school debts amounted in round numbers to $2,000,000,000. The mortgage debt upon real estate reached the sum of $6,000,000,000. Besides, there are the railroad debts and the personal and other debts, so that it may not be an exaggeration to assert that the indebtedness of the American people is not far short of $15,000,000,000.

These debts, in fact, are owed by the people, for the people have to pay them. No man can say that he is out of debt. Each bond is an order for commodities created by human toil. The debts are paid finally in the articles which men produce. Thus, as prices fall, more and more of such articles must be given to meet the requirements of fixed obligation. Men are accustomed to think of buying as an operation performed solely with money. But the farmer who sells his products buys the money as truly as the person to whom he sells them purchases his wares. As prices fall, money becomes continually dearer and demands an increasing sacrifice from him who would procure it for any purpose. The operation of this increase may be indicated by consideration of the following statement, which I did not prepare, but which I believe to be trustworthy :

THE NATIONAL DEBT.

Years.	
In 1866 It was	$2,000,000,000
Paid principal, interest and premium	4,350,000,000
In 1894 Balance due, in dollars, about,	900,000,000

	Bales.
In 1866 It could have been paid in cotton,	14,184,000
Paid principal, interest, etc., in cotton	94,690,000
In 1894 Balance due in cotton at 5 cts.,	51,000,000

	Bushels.
In 1866 It could have been paid in wheat,	1,007,000,000
Paid principal, interest, etc., in wheat	5,022,000,000
In 1894 Balance due in wheat	2,054,900,000

Accepting this statement as accurate, we find that, after paying in cotton nearly seven times the original amount of the national debt, the American people still owe, in cotton, nearly four times the original debt ; and in cotton, wheat and similar materials this debt and all other debts are, as a matter of fact, paid.

When such figures as these are presented, with the appalling fact of the destruction of wealth which they indicate, there is no longer reason for astonishment that, between 1880 and 1895 the number of homes stolen from the people by foreclosure of mortgages (owned by the bankers), amounted to the enormous number of 18,000,000. This can be called by no milder name than Legalized Robbery.—*Heber Clark's Speech Before the Pennsylvania Legislature.*

HISTORY REPEATS ITSELF—WHAT WILL BE THE RESULT IN AMERICA.

Rome was once the grandest and most democratic nation on the earth. Her wealth was then distributed among the multitude, and as a result her people were happy. The land was owned and divided among the millions. Her great soldiers and statesmen were still greater farmers. *Eighty-five* per cent. of the population were land-owners, and knew that they had something to fight for, and as a consequence the Roman soldiers were invincible.

The great German historian, Neibhur, says :

"To what more than to her system of colonization, a branch of her agrarian scheme, was she (Rome) indebted for the security and extension of her frontier? A hosts of warriors were trained up ready to take the field at the call of their country, yet no less ready to exchange the sword for the plow-share. It is not, however, in a military point of view that the value of this institution is evident. They were of no less domestic importance in providing against the phenomena so frequently met with in great cities, of the squalid indingence by the side of the most profuse extravagance."

In one of his most eloquent sermons, the Rev. Gilbert De La Matyer uses the following language :

"With the history of mighty Rome we are all familiar. At the zenith of her real greatness and power, *eighty-five* per cent. of her population held titles in lands, and cultivated their own. Then her people were happy, prosperous, hardy and brave ; her legions were invincible. Then her currency was in volume *one thousand and eight hundred millions ;* when Rome perished, her lands and wealth were in the hands of *two thousand* inviduals.

Dr. Lord says :

"These two thousand persons owned the world ; her currency had been contracted by class legislation to less than *two hundred millions.*"

Allison says :

"The fall of the Roman Empire, so long ascribed to ignorance, slavery, heathenism and moral corruption, was really brought about by a decline in the gold and silver mines of Spain and Greece."

The German historian, Neibhur, from whom I quoted before, says :

"The people gave themselves up in dispair in the fields as beasts of burden lie beneath their load and refused to rise. The disintegration of society was almost complete, all public spirit, all generous emotions, all noble aspirations of man shriveled and disappeared as the *volume of money shrank and prices fell ;* as men decayed wealth accumulated in the hands of the few. Not only did whole provinces (states) become the property of one man. but *usury* existed in so frightful a form that even the virtuous Brutus received sixty per cent. for the use *of* money."

Pliny says :

"These colossal fortunes which ruined Italy were due to *the contraction of estates through usury,* so scarce was money."

Quotations of this character could be pursued much further, but the writer thinks this is sufficient to convince any intelligent person of the real cause of depreciation of value and the *hard times* in our country.

Col. Heath, the late lamented brilliant writer, in one of his newspaper articles truthfully said :

"*Egypt* died when *ninety-seven* per cent. of her wealth became centered in *three* per cent. of her population."

"*Babylon's* fall was caused by *ninety-eight* per cent. of her wealth centering in *two* per cent. of her people."

"*Persia,* the empire of a hundred and seven and twenty provinces (states), kicked the bucket when *one* per cent. of her population had gobbled up the wealth of the realm."

" *Greece*, with more tenacity, succumbed to apoplexy when less than *one* per cent. of her wealth was distributed among *ninety-nine* per cent. of her people.

" *Rome* gave up the ghost when *two thousand* of her nobles owned the world."

" In the American Republic the wealth producers own less than *ten* per cent. of what they have created."

Why did Egypt, Persia, Greece and Rome become decrepit and die? Because they committed suicide by enslaving and starving their working people, through robbing and oppressing them by concentrating the wealth in the hands of the few.

Will the United States follow their example and commit suicide?

Or will it profit from those countries' experience, and avoid their fate?

The American people are almost face to face with three things, despotism, reformation or dissolution. Which will they choose? The writer asks every true, intelligent lover of liberty to carefully consider this example, and do their best to avoid history repeating itself in this rich land. It is not a matter of party lines, but it is the sustaining of our republic and free institutions. As we see daily the moneyed people of our country buying titles of counts, etc., by marriages, and also going to Europe and spending millions to get into aristocratic society. Henry M. Teller, a true, liberty-loving and honest American statesman, and the others, would never have severed their connection with the party of Lincoln (which they helped to organize) if they had not known that the party of Lincoln had passed in the hands of the money sharks that really caused the assassination of the liberator of 4,000,000 slaves in order to enslave black and white to the gold usurers of the world.

AN OBJECT LESSON.

One year's experience with the gold standard shows the general devastation of over $400,000,000 by the official figures of forty-three States, in fact the table and figures show that there is no need of further explanation. The depreciation of value in one year, and it is but a beginning, shows what a continuation of the ruinous gold standard would bring to the great mass of the people. This table is taken from the *Atlanta Constitution*.

STATE.	1893.	1894.	INCREASE.	DECREASE.
Alabama	$260,172,590	$243,771,677		$17,000,913
Arizona	28,468,183	27,061,974		1,406,209
Arkansas	173,526,484	171,965,480		1,597,004
California	1,216,700,000	1,205,918,000		10,782,000
Colorado	238,722,417	208,905,279		29,817,138
Florida	102,965,406	114,246,969	1,281,563	
Georgia	452,644,907	429,012,923		2,363,984
Idaho	33,000,000	28,000,000		5,000,000
Illinois	847,197,516	824,651,628		22,539,888
Indiana	1,302,004,669	1,275,435,377		26,569,292
Iowa	565,857,799	556,412,766		9,445,033
Kansas	356,621,818	337,501,722		19,120,096
Kentucky	706,799,076	696,220,342		10,578,734
Louisiana	250,045,503	251,091,348	1,045,845	
Maryland	524,056,241	529,138,103	5,081,862	
Maine	270,012,782	272,319,370	1,506,588	
Massachusetts	2,791,582,144	2,815,883,621	24,307,477	
Minnesota	642,903,657	648,759,245	5,855,603	
Mississippi	160,916,527	159,058,436		1,891,091
Missouri	994,589,787	999,951,960	5,372,137	
Montana	127,548,175	118,850,892		8,698,088
Nebraska	194,733,124	183,417,498		10,015,622
Nevada	26,178,060	23,628,720		2,544,340
New Hampshire	274,816,342	269,683,799		
New Jersey	768,295,274	774,398,332	6,703,058	
New Mexico	43,630,240	41,128,620		2,501,620
New York	4,038,058,994	4,273,942,431	235,883,482	
North Carolina	261,717,727	262,917,119	1,209,392	
Oklahoma	15,029,927	14,830,495		199,432
Ohio	1,752,990,930	1,742,662,115		10,328,815
Oregon	168,088,905	150,399,383		17,689,522
Pennsylvania	9,115,320,549	3,162,114,251	46,793,702	
South Carolina	170,242,261	173,508,269	3,266,088	
South Dakota	136,032,840	128,046,765		7,986,075
Tennessee	338,731,726	319,822,187		18,909,529
Texas	886,175,305	867,814,305		18,361,090
Utah	117,505,375	99,542,472		17,962,903
Vermont	176,051,365	175,132,912		918,453
Virginia	466,945,118	464,038,922		2,906,196
Washington	285,634,246	228,356,572		57,277,674
West Virginia	222,218,154	220,007,407		2,210,747
Wisconsin	654,000,000	600,000,000		54,000,000
Wyoming	32,356,801	28,198,041		3,155,760
Totals			$337,700,753	$417,180,790

Here we have an object lesson worth studying, the beauties of the gold standard for the money centers.

We find only twelve States out of forty-three which have increased in valuation, $337,700.753, and by deducting the amount of increase from the $477,180,790, decrease we find $79,480,037, a decrease in valuation that we cannot account for. Why? Because the value of wealth was destroyed by the contraction of the currency, which advanced in value, because every time you create contraction the value of money raises thereof.

By studying the figures we find that New York (a money center) alone has $235,883,482 of the increase, or 70 per cent. The next comes Pennsyvania (another money center) with $46,793,702 increase, and Massachusetts, with $24,301,477. So we find that these three States (the money centers of the country) increased their valuation $306,978,761, leaving only $30,731,992 for the other nine States quoted in the increase. When we consider this we cannot come to any other conclusion than to see so plain by the figures that the gold standard is the ruin of all the States except these three, and even at that, the people (the masses I mean) of these three States are not in any better condition than their equal in all other States of the Union, because there is more misery in New York State with $235,883,482 increase than in any other State. The fact is, that the ones which reap the benefit of the gold standard are the *Wall Street Bankers*, and a few other money lenders and *Mortgage Owners*, at the expense of all other people.

Will the voters see?

WORDS FROM WISE MEN.

"A specie-payment system is a contrivance invented to cheat the laboring classes of mankind."—*Daniel Webster.*

The Republican party demands such a system for this country.

"Liberty cannot long endure in any country where the tendency of legislation is to concentrate wealth in the hands of a few.—*Daniel Webster.*

The Republican party started to concentrate wealth in the hands of a few, and Grover Cleveland, the Mugwump, has done the same.

" Whoever controls the volume of money in any country is absolute master of all industry and commerce."—*James A. Garfield.*

The people should not allow the National banks to live long, because they will then control the volume of money more than they do now, as the vampires have in view the retirement of the greenbacks and replace the National bank notes instead in order to perpetuate the system and keep on bonding and robbing the people.

·" The greenback currency, based as it is upon the credit of the nation, is the best money the world ever saw."—*U. S. Grant.*

General Grant hit the nail on the head when he said that, because paper money is the cheapest, lightest and best money in the world, for that reason the bankers want to issue it themselves.

" I affirm it as my conviction that class laws, placing capital above labor in the structure of government, is more dangerous to the Republic than was chattel slavery in the days of its haughtiest supremacy."—*Abraham Lincoln.*

Who to-day, doubts for a moment that the whole legislation in Congress is dictated by capital and corporations for their interest only?

" If a government should contract a debt with a certain amount of money in circulation, and then contracted the money volume before the debt was paid, it would be the most henious crime a government could commit against the people."—*Abraham Lincoln.*

That is just what this government has done, it contracted the war debt, and afterward not only contracted the money volume but destroyed it and funded the debt, and afterward, in 1873, destroyed half of the volume of money and they expect to keep on doing it all the time.

" Labor is prior to and independent of capital. Capital is only the fruit of labor and could never have existed if labor had not first existed. Labor is the superior of capital, and deserves much the higher consideration."—*Abraham Lincoln.*

These words were in a message to the Congress of the United States. Does the legislation of that body for the past thirty years look as though our law-makers believed these words of Lincoln? I quote these words to prove that the Republican party of Lincoln is dead, for the party of that name is now absolutely dominated by capitalists and syndicates.

" If Congress has the right under the Constitution to issue paper money, it was given them to be used by themselves, not to be delegated to individuals or corporations."—*Andrew Jackson.*

The political mercenary tools in Congress have sold out this right to the National banks for good prices, or they are themselves interested in the banks, and they vote for their own interest all the time.

"I am not among those who fear the people. They, and not the rich, are our dependance for continued freedom ; and to preserve their independence, we must not let our rulers load us with perpetual debt."—*Thomas Jefferson.*

Grover Cleveland differs from the founder of democracy and the author of that sacred document, the Declaration of Independence, which freed us from England. Grover now seeks to annul it by enslaving the people to the gold lords of England with an intent to perpetuate the debt.

" I believe that banking institutions are more dangerous to our liberties than standing armies. Already they have set up a money aristocracy that has set the government at defiance. The issuing power should be taken from the banks and restored to the government and the people, to whom it properly belongs. Let the banks exist, but let them bank on coin or treasury notes."—*Thomas Jefferson.*

Here is another very different stand taken by Jefferson, than the one taken in opposition now by the would-be patriots and Democrats of the present Administration. It is true that the Republicans took the cake in favoring the National bankers, but Grover and the clique want to do better and get away with the whole bakery by giving the bankers the sole right to issue money and keep up the aristocracy.

"The national banks are responsible for the destruction of the greenbacks, the payment of the bonds in coin, the funding acts, the demonitization of silver, and all the corrupt financial legislation in this country for the past thirty years. They have boycotted and discriminated against every kind of money that promised relief to the debtor class and prosperity to the industrial masses. They are boycotters of the most cruel and merciless kind."—*Grand Master J. R. Sovereign of the Knights of Labor.*

Yes, you are right Mr. Sovereign, but John Sherman, of Ohio, whom many Americans believe to be a great patriot and financier (?), did all the dirty work necessary to carry into law the acts and schemes of the bankers. He is still at it, and expects to succeed Carlisle should McKinley get elected, whom the chumps will vote for and believe that he is the working

men's friend. Oh yes, they will find out later on. Sherman intends to do great work for the Rothschilds when he gets there. Will he have the chance?

"Fifty men in these United States have it in their power, by reason of the wealth which they control, to come together within twenty-four hours and arrive at an understanding by which every wheel of commerce may be stopped, and every electric key struck dumb. These fifty men can paralyze the whole country, for they can control the circulation of the currency and create a panic whenever they will." *Chauncey M. Depew.*

If Depew never told the truth before, he told it at the time he said this, because it was only ten bankers that created the panic of 1893, and it only takes about double that number to paralyze commerce as things are run only to suit the government of aristocracy nowadays. And they are making threats of panic right now.

"My agency in procuring the passage of the National Bank Act was the greatest financial mistake of my life. It has built up a monopoly that affects every interest in the country. It should be repealed; but, before this can be accomplished, the people will be arrayed on one side and the banks on the other, in a contest such as we have never seen in this country."—*Salmon P. Chase.*

This was said by Mr. Chase shortly before he died. Chase was the Secretary of the Treasury under Mr. Lincoln, whom the bankers had fixed or persuaded to push the National Banking Act, and he told Lincoln he would resign his office if the President did not sign the Act within two hours.

All the greatest men of this country were for both gold and silver and against the gold standard, to wit: Washington, Jefferson, Franklin, Jackson, Lincoln, Grant, Garfield, Blaine and many others. Harrison (who now says he will stump for McKinley) signed the Sherman Silver Purchasing Act, after the bankers had sent 1100 telegrams to veto it, and that was the reason the bankers defeated him. The writer got money from a Republican National bank president of Los Angeles, Cal., to defeat him, and I know what I am talking about. So be patriotic and American above party.

The bankers have always fixed things so as to have the Secretary of the Treasury and Comptroller of the Currency with them, and get the Secretary of Treasury to deposit the money of the people with them so that they can get interest upon it, and

men's friend. Oh yes, they will find out later on. Sherman
intends to do great work for the Rothschilds when he gets there.
Will he have the chance?

" Fifty men in these United States have it in their power, by reason of the
wealth which they control, to come together within twenty-four hours and arrive at
an understanding by which every wheel of commerce may be stopped, and every
electric key struck dumb. These fifty men can paralyze the whole country, for
they can control the circulation of the currency and create a panic whenever they
will."—*Chauncey M. Depew.*

If Depew never told the truth before, he told it at the time
he said this, because it was only ten bankers that created the
panic of 1893, and it only takes about double that number to
paralyze commerce as things are run only to suit the government
of aristocracy nowadays. And they are making threats of panic
right now.

This was said by Mr. Chase shortly before he died. Chase
was the Secretary of the Treasury under Mr. Lincoln, whom the
bankers had fixed or persuaded to push the National Banking
Act, and he told Lincoln he would resign his office if the President did not sign the Act within two hours.

All the greatest men of this country were for both gold and silver and against the gold standard, to wit : Washington, Jefferson,
Franklin, Jackson, Lincoln, Grant, Garfield, Blaine and many
others. Harrison (who now says he will stump for McKinley)
signed the Sherman Silver Purchasing Act, after the bankers had
sent 1400 telegrams to veto it, and that was the reason the
bankers defeated him. The writer got money from a Republican
National bank president of Los Angeles, Cal., to defeat him,
and I know what I am talking about. So be patriotic and
American above party.

The bankers have always fixed things so as to have the
Secretary of the Treasury and Comptroller of the Currency with
them, and get the Secretary of Treasury to deposit the money of
the people with them so that they can get interest upon it, and

also by controlling it, create panics and force bond issues at their will. The old bonds would have expired in 1907, which would have ended the National banking system. They had too good a snap to let it go easily. So they created the panic, and arranged with Cleveland and Carlisle to issue more bonds in order to prolong for thirty years or more their system of usury and legalized robbery. This nation will never get out of debt as long as the National banking law is in the Statute Books of our country, because the banker will do anything to prolong it if they have to spend millions, which they get back double.

God save this country from falling in the hands of Ohio's statesmen. (?) They have been a disgrace in the past, to wit: Salmon P. Chase was twice Governor of Ohio, and the agent who procured the passage of the National Banking Act. Senator Wade who said: " By the gods Johnson (who succeeded Lincoln),

.. .. p...... ... j..p.. ....g .,
Corporation Lawyer Foraker (Senator-elect to do the work for corporations, as Sherman is too old), who worked for the gold platform in St. Louis, and moved to lay on the table Senator Teller's bimetallic substitute, is from Ohio. McKinley, the Hanna trust and syndicate man, is from Ohio. People will find out their mistake if they do not stop it, because the result will be the fulfilling of Lincoln's prophecy (the destruction of this republic), just as sure as Cæsar and the wealthy classes destroyed the grand Roman republic, that cost Cæsar his life. Do you wish to establish a potentate government in this country? , Here is what the potentates get per day, besides other things:

Emperor (Czar) of Russia	$25,000
Sultan (Despot) of Turkey	18,000
Emperor (Bigot) of Austria	10,000
King (Humbug) of Italy	8,600
Emperor William of Germany	8,000
Queen Victoria of England	5,000

Considering the services of those people, are they not over paid? Yes! But these people and the shylocks are protecting their interest? Why is it that the masses do not do the same?

also by controlling it, create panics and force bond issues at their will. The old bonds would have expired in 1907, which would have ended the National banking system. They had too good a snap to let it go easily. So they created the panic, and arranged with Cleveland and Carlisle to issue more bonds in order to prolong for thirty years or more their system of usury and legalized robbery. This nation will never get out of debt as long as the National banking law is in the Statute Books of our country, because the banker will do anything to prolong it if they have to spend millions, which they get back double.

God save this country from falling in the hands of Ohio's statesmen. (?) They have been a disgrace in the past, to wit: Salmon P. Chase was twice Governor of Ohio, and the agent who procured the passage of the National Banking Act. Senator Wade, who said: " *By the gods, Johnson* (who succeeded Lincoln), *we have faith in you, there will not be any trouble now in running the government.*" After Lincoln's death he was leading U. S. Senator from Ohio. John Sherman, "the author of Hard Times," who sold this country, and who will, it is reported, take the stump to endeavor to prevent the people from redeeming it, is from Ohio. Corporation Lawyer Foraker (Senator-elect to do the work for corporations, as Sherman is too old), who worked for the gold platform in St. Louis, and moved to lay on the table Senator Teller's bimetallic substitute, is from Ohio. McKinley, the Hanna trust and syndicate man, is from Ohio. People will find out their mistake if they do not stop it, because the result will be the fulfilling of Lincoln's prophecy (the destruction of this republic), just as sure as Cæsar and the wealthy classes destroyed the grand Roman republic, that cost Cæsar his life. Do you wish to establish a potentate government in this country? Here is what the potentates get per day, besides other things:

Emperor (Czar) of Russia	$25,000
Sultan (Despot) of Turkey	18,000
Emperor (Bigot) of Austria	10,000
King (Humbug) of Italy	8,600
Emperor William of Germany	8,000
Queen Victoria of England	5,000

Considering the services of those people, are they not over paid? Yes! But these people and the shylocks are protecting their interest? Why is it that the masses do not do the same?

HOW THE BANKERS FOOL THE PEOPLE.

Let us see how the Bankers have fooled the people so long and still fool them, and the people do not know yet how it is done, and why the bankers have all they want and good times, while millions of other people and their innocent children and wives starve and freeze and become paupers more and more, while the bankers and money lenders become millionaires.

Here it is in a nut shell, how it is done; about a year or so prior to the election the bankers set their machines to work, the lying and corrupt newspaper-politicians, and they commence writing articles over articles, who should be the best man to nominate for President, etc., the best man for the people of both parties; and they do like the nut-shell swindlers or presto change sure thing man, on the table of sectional hate, they being working and working it yet. The Mason and Dixon Line is their table North and South, Free Trade and Protection, "you know," and with said articles over articles they get the people excited and prejudiced against one another about it, as they are doing now and all the time the same thing, until about a few days before the primaries election for delegates to the convention ; then Mr. Banker sends for the ward heeler or the boss politician, you know him, the fellow that never work hard, but has soft jobs and big pay or does not work at all, but wears good clothes at our expense, and the bankers tell him about the newspaper articles, etc., and who will be the best man to nominate, and who should be the delegates to the convention, and will furnish the money to carry out his plan. The fellow takes it of course, and puts it where it does the most good, in his pocket, except a few dollars to fool the people; the warm-up to treat them and promises great times and good jobs with big pay, and commences his work this way. "Say boys did you see the article in the papers this morning about Mr. C., that was a good article ; was it not ? Mr. C. is no good ; we don't want to nominate him ; we want Mr. Mc., he is a good man and a good candidate and will sweep the country, and we must nominate him ; he is all right, boys, and if we nominate and elect him we will have good times sure. Mr. Barkeeper give us a drink ; come boys all take a drink with

me, and here's looking at you, here's for Mc., here's for Har.,
here's for Reed; give us another drink Mr. Barkeeper, as
they are getting warmed up in great shape," and my friend's
man will get there sure, the Banker's man.

After the first drink; "Now let me tell you, boys, if we
nominate Mr. Mc., we are all right, as he is for good wages,
good times and protection to American labor and plenty of
work, because it protects the American people," and for that
reason we must nominate him; give us another drink; drink
what you want, boys. I want California wine. I take Col.
Booze, of Kentucky, says another that is spilling it already,
and finally he has got them in such shape that they do not
think of their wives and children waiting home, and puts
them in line with torches and marches them to hear the great
L.—Speaker, the Banker's mouth-piece, and they hurrah and
whoop it up for the G. O. P. That night is solid North
Republican and protection to American Labor, good wages
and lots of work and down with Free Trade and the solid
South, and sometimes they fight the war over and knock one
another silly, etc.

GETTING THEM WARMED UP IN GREAT SHAPE

About a week or so after, the Democratic Bankers send for the Democratic Boss Politician, dem-primaries you know, and furnishes him the warm up, may be not so much, but he must have it to go through the same story, and that night is Solid South Democracy and Government by the people and for the people, and down with trusts and the robbers' tariff, etc., etc.

You see one night Solid North and another night (presto-change) Solid South, until the nominations are made ; after the nominations the Bankers go to a summer resort or other places and have good times on the result, as they know now that it is head they win, and tail we lose, which ever way it goes, and leaves them to fight it out until Election Day, and after election the North raises his cover, and presto-change, the great good times, good wages and protection to American Labor are gone.   The South raises his cover, and also the great promises of Government for the people and by the people, and down with monopoly and trusts, are gone (one Sugar Trust got down on the people) and now comes Mr. Banker from behind and raises his cover, and there is his gold that with the vicious laws passed, grows and grows, and everything else down and decreasing, he has the laugh on us all.   Democrats and Republicans he fools, both North and South, on sectional hate, while our interest is intrinsically the same.   Lots of fun for the Banker and you.   See, see!

How the Bankers fool the people. Sectional hate Mason
and Dixon line.

HOW THE "BANKER" GETS THE CROPS, RAIN OR SHINE, OR GETS THE FARM

The contraction and monopoly of our currency for not having the government issue it, and not having sufficient medium of exchange (money) in circulation according to the demand, and how the Bankers get the benefit.

Now we take a city with a farmer, a merchant, a miller, a banker, etc. ; the farmer has a good farm and wishes to seed it ; he is out of debt, and has everything—horses, plows, seed, etc., but he has not the money to pay his help or get provisions. We say he has the above mentioned properties, but how many farmers have not even that. He wishes to seed his farm and he asks his neighbor if he can loan him $1,000. "No, I have not got it John, I had some money and I put it in the bank, and it failed and I lost it." (And there is where the people put the money in these days, and the bankers get the interest on the people's money, and sometimes get it all). So Mr. John has to start for the bank where the money is and our government has given Mr. Banker the monopoly, and even the people keep there what little they have, and there goes Mr. John, the farmer, to the bank. Mr. Clerk comes "What can I do for you, Mr. John." "I wish to borrow some money to seed my farm." "Will you please wait a few minutes, the President or the Cashier will talk to you." Mr. President comes—"What can I do for you, John." "I wish to borrow $1,000 on my ranch to seed it." "Oh, money is very tight with us just now and I don't think that we can accommodate you, Mr. John." That is the first statement they make to John. "Well, gentlemen, I must have $1,000 to seed my farm which is clear of mortgages, etc., and I have the seed, etc., only need the money. I have been a good customer of the bank for many years, too." "Well, come in to-morrow, we will consider the matter and try to accommodate you" they say to him. Now they consult and see how much interest they should charge him. "Oh, those farmers make plenty of money with their crops," said the Cashier. Well we will charge him 12 per cent if he wants the money ; he says he must have it," answers the President. "So much the

better, then," says the Cashier, "and see that the papers or
mortgage and notes are all drawn straight by our lawyers"
(the best in town, you know). John comes the next day and
asks if they have concluded to accommodate him. "Yes,
Mr. John," says the Clerk; "I had a hard time to persuade
them to make the loan, as money is very tight, you know,
and we have to charge you 12 per cent and you to pay the
cost of drawing the papers, etc., if you wish the loan." It
is too much interest, but what can the farmer do; he has to
have the money or not seed the ranch. So the papers are
drawn and recorded and John gets the money—about $850 after
the interest and other expenses are taken off, and he goes to
work and seeds his ranch, we say with wheat, but it applies to
every other crop raised, and he has to take all the chances of
scarcity of rain, of too much rain, that floods his crops, of
storms coming and destroying it, or other elements that he
cannot help; but not a single chance is taken by the cold-
blooded and sure-thing Banker; he has a first mortgage on
the farm and the crops. But suppose we say this time the
farmer is lucky and he gets a good crop—now the time is
getting near to pay the mortgage and he has to hustle and get
his crops to market or the Banker will foreclose on him; so he
puts his wheat in the wagon and goes to town to sell it and he
sees the merchant. "Say, Jack, do you want to buy some
wheat? I will sell it to you cheap so that you can make
money on it." "How cheap, John?" 40c. a bushel, and it is
the best wheat you ever saw; come and look at it outside in
the wagon." Jack sees the wheat and it is good and he would
like to buy it, but he is in the same fix as John was (contraction you know brings the money where it starts from).
"I tell you John what I will do I will trade with you," says
Jack. "No, no Jack, I have to have money to pay out, and
the fellows I owe it to do not want goods." "I know it, but
I will do my trading with you some other time, and I will
patronize you if you patronize me," and so as Jack likes the
wheat and wants to get John's trade and wishes to speculate
with John, he says wait "I will see if I can buy it," and he goes
to the bank, may be some other bank, but a bank anyway.
"Gentlemen, I have a chance to buy John's wheat cheap and
it is good, and I am short of money just now; I paid some

heavy bills and I would like to borrow $1,200." "Money is very tight with us just now"—same old story—"but if you have a chance to make money we will accommodate you, being an old customer of the bank, but we have to charge a little more interest than usual." "How much," asks Jack. "Oh, 12 per cent, you know you will make money and you will make it with our money and get John's trade, too." "All right," says Jack Another mortgage on the merchant's property and he gets the money, buys the wheat and pays John and John returns it back to the bank where it started from.

Now the merchant has the wheat and he holds it to see if prices will go up so that he may make something on it, but the time gets near when his note will be due and he has to hustle too or the Banker will have a Sheriff lock on his door, and Jack hunts up Peter the miller. "Say, Peter, I have good wheat I bought cheap from John when he needed money. I would like to sell it now. Come and look at it." Peter goes. "See, Peter, fine wheat, just as good as gold" says Jack (who does not know that it is better than gold—can we eat gold). Peter likes it, and they agree on the price as Jack needs money now, and Peter goes and borrows from the bank, pays Jack and Jack returns it to the bank where it started from. We leave the baker alone; say he buys a small quantity and pays cash or weekly, but before that bread is eaten by the consumers it has paid three interests, 36 per cent to the Banker, which the consumer must pay for—and does the Banker work for it? Usurers and Shylocks repeal the National Banking Act. Issue the money by the government and the Banker cannot rob the people and cannot create panics and force legislation in their favor to issue more bonds and perpetuate this robbery.

CITY OF "BANKERS' COUNTRY."

How the Bankers get the Crops, rain or shine, or get the Farm.

THE LAW AND HOW DIFFERENTLY IT IS AD-MINISTERED BY OUR COURTS, OR MADAME JUSTICE, AND HOW SHE APPEARS WHEN SAME IS TO BE ADMINISTERED.

These are facts, and on record, and we are all familiar with them, and no one can call me to account that our laws are violated by Capitalists and Corporations and there is no punishment for them, while on the other hand the poor are declared guilty in advance and before trying their cases, by pseudo law abiding citizens and defiers of the law of the land. Let us prove this assertion.

On August 5th, 1892, Congress passed a law authorizing the outright gift of $2,500,000 of the people's money as Souvenir Coin to the Columbian Exposition Company, a corporation of Chicago Capitalists, and in order to effect the passage of said law the said corporation of Chicago Capitalists accepted and agreed to allow a clause to be added (so plain for any one to understand it) closing the World's Columbian Exposition on Sunday. And the corporation was paid $2,500,000 to obey that law of Congress, which was passed by a majority of 48 and was signed by President Harrison on the same day, and they took that money on those conditions, but they did not obey the law. After three Sunday closings of said Exposition, or on May 12th, 1893, the Legislative Committee of the directors of said corpora-tion, composed of Edwin Walker (chairman), Ferd. W. Peck, F. S. Vinton and Arthur Dixon, as his associates, reported and deliberately said Congress had no power to pass such a law (but they took the money on that condition). The directors of said corporation, Lyman J. Gage, Davis, Hutchinson, McNally, Kerfoot and Lawson, acting upon said report from the Legislative Committee and declaring themselves the champion law-makers of the land. On May 16th, 1893, under the rules of said corporation they ordered the Fair opened on Sunday, against the protests of the National Commissioners, and some of said Commissioners advocated that the general government would be applied to for the sending of troops to close said Fair, to no avail, as the Administrative Committee of said Fair, under the rules, opened the gates of the Fair and defied the law on May 28, 1893. What was the result? The government brought suit against said corporation to obey the law and close the Fair, and on June 8th a temporary Injunction was granted to the United States District Attorney Milchrist, but when the case went before the U. S. Court, Chief Justice Fuller of the U. S. Supreme Court, Justice Bunn of Wisconsin and Allen of Illinois, decided the case against the Government and in favor of the corporation. Edwin Walker was the Attorney for the corporation (in which he was interested). And after it did not pan out as they wanted, they were saying they wanted to give a chance to the Workingmen of Chicago to see the Fair, but they cared more for the 50c. of the workingmen than all the workingmen of the world. What they were after was the 50c., so the workingmen did not patronize Sunday opening, and all the foreign exhibits were covered, and the press outside of Chicago, and especially the religious press, started to boycott the Fair. The directors, on July 14th, 1893, in order to clear themselves of moral obligation, rescinded their order to open the Fair, and on July 22nd the Council of Administration ordered the Fair closed, which was done the next day, Sunday July 23rd. They did as they pleased ; disobeyed the laws of Congress and the orders of the U. S. Courts.

One Chas. W. Clingman did better than the government on law enforcing, and had the directors fined for contempt of court before Judge Stein, Mr. Davis was fined $250 and the others $1,000 each.

Here comes another important case that we all also know; the A. R. U., not a corporation but workingmen that tried to protect themselves from starving and striked. Debs, Howard, Keliher, Rogers and others, in which Mr. Edwin Walker of the World's Fair fame was the Special Attorney to prosecute those people (and he says in advance according to an associated press dispatch, sent broadcast all over the land) guilty in advance of the trying of their case "we want Debs and every man that has trampled on the law to be punished," and he was a mascot, as Federal Judge William A. Woods sentenced them to six months each, but at least if Debs and his associates violated the Interstate Commerce Law they surely did not get $2,500,000 and then break the law.   Here is what Mr. Walker is supposed to have said :

THEY WANT DEBS.

National Government Will Punish all the Strike Leaders.

Chicago, July 5.—"If the strike was settled to-day it would not make any difference," said Edwin Walker, special counsel for the Government.   "Every man who has trampled on the law will be punished.   I do not care anything about the few misguided men who have been arrested.   It is the instigator of the lawlessness that the Government wants to punish.   That is Debs.   We shall have Debs.   We have the evidence against him now, and he will be punished."

A special grand jury to sit next Tuesday was summoned this morning.—*Cincinnati Tribune*, July 6, 1894.

Debs and the others went in jail.

It reminds the writer of the Tyrant Emperor Tiberius, of the Roman Empire, when he was decreeing so many laws and wanted them strictly obeyed, but his majesty's empolyes were violating them by the wholesale, and one day Tiberius, asked his Prime Minister Tacitus what he thought of the last law that he, Tiberius, had decreed, and Tacitus philosophically answered and said: "Your Majesty, to tell you the truth about the matter, you are decreeing so many laws that it is impossible to execute them, and your own lawyers and judges do not obey them.   What can you expect from the other people that see the examples" (good for Tacitus, he was for good examples).   Tiberius was assassinated.

The writer could quote hundreds of such cases all over the land, See Editorial of the *Chicago Times* about the Santa Fe R. R. (Page.113)Here is an example while I was in Cincinnati. Food Inspector Pendergast arrested a poor milkman for having put a little water in the milk that he was selling; he was convicted, fined and sent to the Workhouse.

The R. R. and other corporations water their stocks very heavy and what do they get for punishment?   The best

seats in the U. S. Senate and House of Representatives. See
the difference in the Law and Madame Justice as she appears
when Justice is to be delivered, quite different you know.

MADAME JUSTICE, AND HOW SHE APPEARS WHEN JUSTICE IS TO BE DELIVERED.

The Law and how different it is Administered
in our Country.

The $100,000,000 gold reserve in the United States
Treasury is without any law, for it was established by John
Sherman when he was Secretary of the Treasury in 1875. No
need for it but only kept there for the bankers to gamble on.
They made the Secretary of the Treasury make a hole in it
and run it down to 40 or 50 millions, by paying the expenses
of the government in gold, when he can pay them in silver, as
the law says in coin and gives the Secretary the power to use
his discretion about it. Now by paying the expenses in gold
it makes a hole in the gold reserve and the bankers commence
to say your credit is running down and you had better issue
some bonds and fill the hole, and the Government, do issue

bonds and fill it. Then the Secretary digs another hole and
again the same old story; your credit is running down, issue
more bonds and fill the hole, and by making and filling the
holes God knows when they will stop issuing bonds.

Is the credit of a man or of a government that keeps
$100,000,000 in gold lying idle in his safe (only there for
bankers to speculate with) any better than another man or
government that instead of keeping the $100,000,000 idle in
the safe has it invested in good paying properties that
bring him revenue and keeps it increasing and furnishes
employment to his fellow citizens and so increases wealth?
That man or government is a progressive one, while the
other is not.

Now if the One hundred million dollars gold reserve were
used and put in such properties as Railroad and Telegraph
lines that ought to be owned by the government, it would
bring revenue to the government and employ citizens of the
said government (and it is the duty of every civilized government to take care of its citizens if said government wishes to
exist, and it is said that a friend in need is a friend indeed)
and stop strikes, and no extortionate rate would be charged for
transportation of any matter by Railroad or Telegraph lines,
or even so it would go back to the people.   No paralelling
of Railroads to freeze out small concerns and freezing out
of small stockholders. The post-office and the telegraph
ought to be combined together. The government or the people
of the United States have done more for the developing of the
telegraph invention than the owners, as the government gave
Professor Samuel F. B. Morse $30,000 on March 3rd, 1843, for
an experiment of his invention, by the passage of the telegram
bill, and the invention was tried and it proved a success on the
first telegram, which was sent on Friday, May 24th, 1844, at
8.45 A. M. from Washington to Baltimore.   After it proved a
success the money power commenced to grab it, but before that
they were saying Morse was crazy and he had to work from
1832 to 1843 to get the government to help him out as no
capitalist or corporation would take chances (The government
or the people have given too much money and also land grants
to enrich a few men and it is about time to stop and have

government ownership of Railroads and Telegraph lines, and stop strikes trouble and killing of people.

It has been the defect and contraction of our currency for not having the government issue it according to business demands that has made it easy for the moneyed men of England to buy our best paying properties and no wonder gold finds its way to England. There are 9 million of mortaged homes in the United States that the money sharks are going to grab, and they are cutting wages to starvation and causing strikes trouble and increasing crime in our land.

The Tariff Question is a sectional hate scheme, and it is used by the bankers only to keep the people in the dark concerning the main and vital question, the money question, and keep the people divided in sectional hate and prejudiced, fighting one another. Now if the United States government protects one citizen it has to protect the others, or if it protects the State of Louisiana with her rice, sugar, etc., it must protect California with her oranges, grapes etc., and so on with every State and their industries, as they are all entitled to the same protection under the same government; protect all or none. And by our government having protected certain citizens it created dissension and just prejudice by the non-protected ones, and the bankers and money power have got in their fine work and got away with the money question and vicious laws. The money question if properly agitated will unite the people from Maine to California and from the Canadian line to the Gulf of Mexico, as all the American people will be and are interested in it, and they see now the suffering on that account, so interest yourself in the most important question that has and is yet agitating the world, the money question. Remember that the bankers have no scruples and will do it every time and they have ruined great and powerful nations of this earth whenever they had a chance or a foothold. They will ruin ours if we let them go on, so let us stop them if we are sincere and true Americans.

WHILE HONEST MEN QUARREL, BANKERS HAVE GOT IN THEIR FINE WORK.

The Tariff question and how it is used by the Bankers.

PRESIDENT CLEVELAND ON SILVER.

Here are the three last paragraphs of his message of March 29th, 1894, vetoing the Bland Bill for the coinage of fifty-five millions of silver seignorage in our treasury.

This leads me to earnestly present the desirability of granting to the secretary of the treasury a better power than now exists to issue bonds to protect our gold reserve when for any reason it should be necessary. Our currency is in such a confused condition and our financial affairs are apt to assume at any time so critical a position that it seems to me such a course is dictated by ordinary prudence.

I am not insensible to the arguments in favor of coining the bullion seigniorage now in the treasury, and I believe it could be done safely and with advantage, if the secretary of the treasury had the power to issue bonds at a low rate of interest under authority in substitution of that now existing, and better suited to the protection of the treasury.

I hope a way will present itself in the near future for the adjustment of our monetary affairs in such a comprehensive and conservative manner as will afford to silver its proper place in our currency, but in the meantime I am extremely solicitous that whatever action we take on this subject may be such as to prevent loss and discouragement to our people at home and the destruction of confidence in our financial management abroad.

GROVER CLEVELAND.

EXECUTIVE MANSION, *March* 29, 1894.

Mr. Cleveland says that Congress should give more power to the Secretary of the Treasury, (which has too much power now) to issue bonds at small rates of interest, so that we can then coin the silver bullion in the treasury; but if Congress does not give such power we cannot coin it, and he vetoes it. If we pay interest we can, if we do not pay interest we can't, you see.

Which private citizen or concern would go to work and issue his interest paying note to another man (an outsider) for the privilege of using his own or their material, that he or they have in their store. Would you do it? Certainly not. Now, the people have the Silver Bullion in the Treasury and want to have it coined so as to use it; and Congress passed the Bland Seignorage silver Coining Bill; the Senate passed it too. Mr. Banker sees Mr. Cleveland and tells him that we have to issue bonds to pay them the interest and then we can coin and use it, but if we don't pay them interest we cannot use it, and Mr. Cleveland vetoes it; and he is for bonds because he knows the reason why, there is something loose somewhere. God may bless you Mr. President, but don't flatter yourself that you can play patriot or democrat, because you do not know how and your own actions show it.

POINTS FOR THE PEOPLE.

Lincoln was the President of the people and he opposed any scheme that tended to rob them· He also was against the usurers and was assassinated. Christ was a bi-metallist and preached against usurers and for the elevation of mankind. He was crucified for it. But look to-day what the world thinks of them, and you will not be able to withstand preaching the same as they did, and God will be with you. Why not? This is a cause of humanity vs. oppression.

When there is enough money in circulation it will start plenty of work, and the result will be good times and prosperity for all, because the working people are the ones who spend and put their money into circulation as soon as they get it.

From 1791 (when gold and silver were made the unit of value) up to 1873, when this nation was nothing compared with to-day's strength, the illustrious patriots did not need to ask or wait for the consent of any other nation. A free, self government that has to obtain the consent of a foreign power before it can legislate vital laws for its people is no longer a free, self government but a subservient government not worth having.

Such has been the case with this government since 1873, and it is still evident with the narrow-minded or interested leaders in the present financial imbroglio. Not only do they not know what they want in the way of legislation for the relief of the people, but, according to the doctrines in vogue, they have to secure first the good will of England or the Rothschilds (which will never be given) and then legislate.

When John Bull adopted the gold standard in 1816 (three years after the defeat of Napoleon) he did not care a continental for the consent of any other nation. He acted in accordance with his own sweet will and for the benefit of England, which is a creditor nation and whose best interest is served by keeping up the gold standard so as to control the world, which is against her. Her fall is not far distant. What is the use, then, for the United States to be a country of enormous strength, wealth and resources? If we would only lead in finances, others would surely follow; but to do this we should not believe in and be led by the chicken-hearted politicians and newspapers under the control of the money sharks.

Cleveland made one of his bluffs (in order to avoid criticism
on his last bond sale) with his Venezuela message, which nearly
put this country in a position which meant nothing less than a
stupid war when we were not prepared, possessing only a small
standing army and an embryotic navy. The Monroe Doctrine is
most respectable, *but it is criminal to use it as a machine for the
benefit of the money brokers.* The people were deceived at first, but
better sense prevailed. That we must and shall fight England
there is not the least doubt, but it is not on land or sea we must
annihilate the British Lion, but attack it in its stronghold—the
control of the world's finances. The Britishers are after our land
and resources. That is what they want. Let us come to the
rescue and keep up the prices by having more money in circulation through bi-metallism and retaining the control of our products and properties. England will have to starve or come to
terms. This is the true solution, and there is no necessity of
going to Venezuela.

When the free coinage of gold and silver at the present ratio
of 16 to 1 is started, this country will begin an era of prosperity
never equalled in her history, and it will force England into bi-
metallism too, because the Latin Union will join with us and
England and Germany will be put into a position whereby they
will be the loosers, as it will give the advantage to the countries
adopting bi-metallism of receiving the difference on exchange,
and they will soon see into it. This is the true way to universal
bi-metallism.

The money lenders of the whole world say, that with more
money in circulation the price of products (necessaries of life)
will rise, and as they *generally are non-producers*, they oppose the
increase of money. Why? Because they want to get products
of Labor at their own prices and then squeeze the producer.
They know what is good; you don't. The Bankers know what
a good thing is, and they want it. Now, is it not a good thing to
take care of, use and get away with other people's money? They
swindle, menace and keep down the masses with their own weap-
ons (the money which the people keep in the banks), which they
allow the bankers to have and use, and they do use it with de-
cisive effect.

If you do not wish to enslave your children and yourself, and
make money, write at once to the author of this book for terms,

then *spread the light* and get your friends to buy a copy and read it. They will know then how they have been robbed and what makes the hard times, no work and deprivation. Suppose something would happen that would destroy all the gold there is in the world out of the earth, would the world stop from existing? No, certainly not. The sun would rise and warm the earth, and cabbage "head" and cucumbers will grow as before. Yet there are plenty of intelligent (?) people who believe that the world cannot transact business without gold as money. Why is it that the bankers want the government to coin money of gold and they have the issuing of paper money? It is because the money sharks of the world can corner (monopolize) gold, of which there is not enough for the smallest nation to do business with, but they want to issue the paper money, because no one can ever corner it, as there is too much of it, provided the government will allow them to do so. Also, because paper is cheap, light to carry and answers the purposes. As a matter of business and economy, let us illustrate: If you needed money, or say a bucket; there were three kinds of bucket in the market, one of gold, $5.00; one of silver, $2.50, and one of paper, 25 cents— any of them would do the work and answer the purpose—which one would you buy? The world is getting so enlightened and machinery of every kind is improving all industries, but few people of the world want to go backward and contract the circulating medium of exchange (currency), instead of expanding it, according to demands. Why? Rothschilds & Co. said they want to own the world and all the people in it. Will the people allow him to do it?

Bimetallism will drive the many idle people from the cities to the country to work. The result will be less misery, less crime, less injustice and finally the elevation of mankind, for which Christ sacrificed His young life. What is the matter with religious preachers, are they mortgaged too? A better opportunity than now to do good will never present itself. Why don't they grasp it?

Touch a man's pocketbook or tell him the truth about his crookedness and he will surely squeal and say you are a crank, an anarchist and many other obnoxious names. Is that good argument? No. That is exactly the case now with the law-

protected crooks that criticise the people who composed the
Chicago Convention. England's newspapers said they were cowboys. Why? Because her agents, who went there, could not
do as they have done before, and as a result, all those interested
with her say stop the anarchist, because they want to refuse to
pay us tribute any longer. Will you listen to them? Oh,
Crank, Lunatic, Silver Crazy, etc., is this good argument? Give
me the monopoly of the currency of any country, and take everything else, in fifty years I will own it.

There were two farmers, prior to 1873, supplying the corn for
the chickens of this country. One raised yellow and the other
white corn. As a result there were two kinds of corn on the
market. If the farmer with the yellow corn wanted too much
for his corn the chickens would buy and use white corn, which
answered the purpose, and the owner would raise more to supply
the customers. The farmer with the yellow corn sent his man
to Capitol Hill with plenty of yellow corn, and fed a few big
roosters, and they didn't do a thing but quietly stop all the
chickens from having plenty of white corn to eat. No good,
says the roosters; yellow corn the best to eat. The chickens
began starving, and the farmer with the yellow corn is getting
so fat out of the poor chickens' many eggs that he is ready to
burst out of his clothes. The chickens got together in Chicago
and put forward a good fighting rooster, named White, to boss
the show for them and see that the chickens would not be robbed
any longer of plenty of corn, white and yellow, and lay plenty
of eggs again by taking the monopoly off of the good corn. The
yellow corn farmer hired all the roosters to sing for him and to
stop the white corn man from seeding and raising a crop and
coming round with his corn again. The chickens did not believe those roosters. No, they got together for the first time, saying opposition is the life of trade, and the chickens got and are
getting so many good roosters on their side that when November
comes there will not be none left for the yellow corn agent of
Ohio to celebrate with. The chickens mean business this time.
They want plenty of corn, and they are going to have it. They
secured a farmer boy from a good corn-raising State too. He
can beat all other roosters singing. As soon as the chickens

heard him sing, they wanted and got him. Oh wait and see all the boys' roosters go to the rescue of the poor, good chickens that lay the eggs for all, and it will be a great song for more corn, more fun, more Democrats, more prosperity. Plenty of corn, white and yellow. Victory—doo-doodle-dee-doo is the song,

The Irish National Convention, held at Chicago last October, resolved to use every means to cripple England. Now is the right time for our Irish-Americans to do it by voting against the syndicate which will own the candidate of the gold standard that England has foisted on to the civilized world for her agrandise-ment, and by means of which she is enabled to keep Ireland in bondage. Now is the time for every Irish-American to do it.

Bryan is a friend of Ireland and an enemy of England. Did you see what the English papers had to say about him and the Chicago Convention? Cowboys, anarchists and repudiators. Poor, old England. The Irish will go for you this time. They cannot be fooled any more.

The money power press and the English gold lords, with the American Tories, who rob the American people and spend the stolen money in England, are again trying to create sectionalism and plunge us into a civil war again. Suppress the first one that talks sectionalism to you, if you are a true American patriot. It was England's scheme in 1861–65 to divide us, and that was the reason she helped the South and would have recognized them if only one great battle in the North, such as that of Gettysburg, had been decisively won by her. Be a patriot and not a tool of an enemy in disguise. The calling of hard names by the gold mortgage sharks does not give them votes, and it only shows that they have no ground for argument.

Germany adopted the gold standard after she got six billions of francs in gold from France as indemnity of war in order to make it increase in value. About the same time a bill was passed in Congress, by trickery, demonetizing silver, which no one seems able to account for.

How was silver demonetized? By what method were the United States put upon a gold basis? Did any of the old party platforms twenty odd years ago demand the change? Not at all. The Act of 1873 was passed "silently;" a more suitable

word would be stealthily.   In evidence I quote from the " Con‾
gressional Record : "

> " Mr. Beck : What I complain of, and what I think I have proved, is that the
> House never knew what was in that bill." (First session of the Fiftieth Congress.
> Senate.)

Senator Bogy, of Missouri, uttered the following words in a
speech made in the Senate, June 27, 1876 :

> "; Why the Act of 1873, which forbids the coinage of the silver dollar, was
> passed, no one at this day can give a good reason." ("Congressional Record,"
> Vol. 4, part 5, Forty-fourth Congress, first session, page 4178.)

Senator Hereford, in the Senate, on February 15, 1878, in the
discussion of the demonetization of silver, said :

> "So that I say beyond the possibility of a doubt (and there is no disputing it)
> that bill which demonetized silver, as it passed, never was read, never was dis‾
> cussed, and the chairman of the committee who reported it (who offered the sub‾
> stitute), said to Mr. Holman, when inquired of, that it did not affect the coinage in
> any way whatever." (*Ibid*, page 989.)

Mr. Holman, in a speech delivered in the House of Representatives July 13, 1876, said :

> "I have before me the record of the proceedings of this House on the passage of
> that measure, a record of which no man can read without being convinced that the
> measure and the method of its passage through the House was a ' colossal swindle.'
> I assert that the measure never had the sanction of this House, and it does not pos-
> sess the moral force of law." ("Congressional Record," Vol. 4, part 6, Forty-
> fourth Congress, first session, appendix page 193.)

Senator Allison, on February 15, 1878, when the bill (H. R.
1093) to authorize the free coinage of the silver dollar was under
consideration, said :

> "But when the secret history of this bill of 1873 comes to be told, it will dis-
> close the fact that the House of Representatives intended to coin both gold and
> silver, and intended to place both metals upon the French relation instead of upon
> our own, which was the true scientific position with reference to this subject in 1873,
> but that the bill afterwards was doctored."

Senator Stewart, of Nevada, on April 29th, 1896, when in
open Senate, calling Senator Sherman, of Ohio, "the author of
hard times," said :

> "The original Act in 1873 was passed through strategy and fraud.   The
> clause which demonetized silver was not read in the Senate during the discussion of
> the bill.   It is a remarkable fact that no mention was made during the pendency of

the Mint Act which demonetized silver, that the silver dollar was omitted from the list of coinage. The Senator from Ohio (Sherman) had charge of the bill and never alluded to the fact that he was demonetizing silver or adopting the gold standard. If he had done so, his object would have been defeated."

Quotations of this character could be pursued much further, but the American people ought to know by this time that they need more money in circulation to transact the increasing business, and they never will get it by contracting the currency (adopting the gold standard). France paid her war debt to Germany before it became due, surprising old Bismarck, who said :

"The greatest mistake in my life was to not ask more than six billion francs. I thought she would never be able to pay it in such a short time."

The French people went to the rescue of their country and paid the debt, and France owes it to Frenchmen, her people. She is to-day the most prosperous nation on earth. She has $38 per capita circulating medium, while we only have $21.30, including the $784,000,000 in the treasury, which is not in circulation, and when we consider our land wealth and resources in comparison with that of France, we ought to have $250.00 per capita. The articles to be exchanged increases every day, and money (the medium of exchange) should increase also to facilitate commerce.

England is getting away with everything we have nowadays, while the fathers of this country revolted against her for only 20 cents on tea, the would-be patriots are asleep. Wm. Gladstone, in his last speech in Parliament, said :

"England is the greatest creditor nation of the world. All other nations are in debt and owe England $22,000,000,000 in gold, and it is to England's interest to keep up the gold standard for our benefit."

Considering this, it does not appear that England is going to agree to bimetallism until she is forced to it and sees that she will be the looser, which will be the case as soon as this country starts it. France, Italy and Spain will follow and England and Germany then will come into line, too.

The United States produces more gold than any other country in the world, and, according to the system in vogue, it seems that we go down deep in the earth to dig the yellow metal for the sole purpose of sending it to Rothschilds, who always want more.

Now, we will suppose the Government wishes to build a deep-water harbor at San Pedro, California (where they need one), for the commerce of Southern California, and Congress passes an act authorizing the Secretary of the Treasury to issue certificates of deposit to pay them for labor and material, and make them a full legal tender for all debts, public and private, the harbor is the basis of that currency, and all the people and all the wealth of this Nation are the security. Does anyone say that they are not good? Explain if the present system of issuing bonds is any better.

Here is how the bankers drain the gold from the people and from the Treasury. The merchants go and deposit their money in the banks; the bankers assort it and keep all the Treasury Notes redeemable in gold, and keep whatever gold the merchants may bring, and pay the merchants back with bank notes and silver certificates, the merchants think they have the same amount of money, and don't think or knows that the bankers plays that kind of a joke every time that they deposit and draw their money, and the bankers make the profits or let gold become scarce and create panics to force Legislation, and sometimes lock up the bank and go to Canada. See?

Establish Government Banks on the Post Office plan, then the people's money will be safe, as the Government cannot fail or go to Canada. The people will then borrow from the people, and even if they pay 4 or 5 per cent interest it goes back to the people and not to England.

GOLD MONEY IN TIME OF WAR

The man who has accumulated gold money, when the country is in danger of war, packs up his gold and gets out of the danger of being killed. If he had paper money he would stay and fight for his country so as to save his money, that would be lost if the country was whipped and a new Government established.

A banker or money lender will take your paper and let you have money, provided your paper is backed by good property or labor; the interest is what he is after. Do not let them fool you any longer—they cannot fool me.

A friend in need is a friend indeed. Is our government a

friend of the people or a friend of England ? We need more circulating medium and England says no, and our government says no.

Cleveland reviewed the actions of a past administration and said it was wrong to recognize a Republican form of government and he was going to correct the wrong. If the Senate had stood in with him he would down a Republican form of government and seat a nigger queen in the Sandwich Islands. Does the constitution give him such power ? according to his ideas and the way he goes at it he could have gone far back and reviewed the acts of Thomas Jefferson and say that Jefferson had done wrong in writing the Declaration of Independence, and he would go and correct such wrong and turn us over to the Queen and the Gold Lords of England that he is trying to please. * *

The Chicago platform on which he was elected says "First repeal of the Sherman Act;" further on it says "For the coinage of gold and silver without discrimination." He fulfilled one part of the contract but refused to fulfill the other part, and he has deceived democracy. Cleveland would make a good poker player, as he knows how to bluff. after he said what he did about the Brice, Gorman or Wilson bill, (party perfidy and dishonor, etc.,) he would not veto it, but made it become a law to give the Sugar Trust the chance to get their sugar in from Germany that was in the way coming here free of duties, and give the Whisky Trust a chance to get all the whisky they could get out of bond and save 3Cc. a gallon. See what he said about the Bland Silver Bill when he vetoed it. These are Mr. Cleveland's own actions. I have no grudge against the President, but if he has made mistakes it is his own fault.

Those paid newspapers and politicians that are talking against an Income Tax for being a class legislation that affects the rich—why don't they say anything about repealing the National Banking Law ? Is not that law a class legislation ?

Issue paper money from five dollars up and let silver take the place of small change from five dollars down.

The only available strike is to strike at election day and retire the money power and corporation's tools forever, elect laborer and friend of labor, and then they will call the militia out and enforce the laws for the benefit of all and not for the benefit of capital.

DESTROY GREENBACKS IS THE LATEST NEWS FROM LOMBARD STREET, LONDON.

NATIONALIZE RAILROADS AND STOP RUNNING THEM FOR "DIVIDENDS."

The great daily of Chicago, the *Times*, is fighting valiantly for the people's interests. Of the New York bankers, who are thirsting for a new issue of bonds, it says :

> They must not pretend, when they buy the next issue of bonds, which of course, Mr. Cleveland will issue, that they are actuated by motives of the purest patriotism. It is bad enough to be robbed without having the robber profess to be doing a service when he relieves you of your watch and wallet.

Of the Pullman boycott it says :

> The effort of the American Railway union to break the power of the Pullman corporation for the everlasting good of organized labor is chivalric, bold and right.
> In this effort the union should have the co-operation of every organization of railway men.
> The railroads intend to try to make this struggle a Waterloo for organized labor. If they succeed trainmen, firemen, engineers or other railroad employees will find the collar of the corporation made a little tighter about their necks.
> If Messrs. Wilkinson, Sargent and Arthur attempt to interfere to the injury of the Railway union, they will be playing the cause of organized labor false.

It means something when a leading daily comes over to the people so fearlessly as that. Buy of your friends, workingmen, and boycott your enemies and stick together. That is the way to win.

The Assassination of President Carnot startled and shocked the civilized world, the same world that greets with thunderous applause the news of a battle where thousands upon thousands of brave men are pierced with bullet or bayonet, or torn into fragments by cannon balls ; the same world that looks on with cold and heartless indifference, while millions of men, women and children are dying by inches of slow starvation in the midst of unparalled abundance. Queer thing is human nature.—Editorial *Cincinnattian*, June 30th, 1894.

THE FIAT OF THE LAW.

It Makes Gold Worth One Hundred Cents that Cost Only Twenty-two Cents.

Having spent a good deal of time myself in years gone by, sailing against "fiat" money, I have a great deal of fellow feeling for my brothers who are still so much in the dark as to keep on doing what I did. That any government can legislate absolute or intrinsic value into a piece of paper or nickel, or copper, or silver, does seem absurd, don't it? And certainly it also seems absurd to say that the government can legislate value into gold. And yet somehow it contrives to do it. Gold that costs 22 cents to mine in Colorado, in some way gets to be worth a dollar, by the time the Government has stamped it. It becomes valuable, as other things do, by the operation of the laws of supply and demand. There is a demand for money to make exchanges. Under the present economic system we can't do all our business by barter and we must have some representative of value. Government provides such a representative in the shape of legal tender coin and paper. If there wasn't any demand for this the government fiat wouldn't give it any value. And if there wasn't any limit to the supply it wouldn't have any appreciable value. But, with a general demand for money to carry on business and a supply strictly limited, money has value in exchange—not intrinsic value. It is the fiat of the government in making money of either kind legal tender that gives it this value. So two silver dollars, the metal in which is worth in the market only as much as that in one gold dollar, still exchange for as much as two gold dollars. And so a paper dollar, the material in which is worth only a very small fraction of a cent, will exchange for as much as either a silver or a gold dollar.

Now suppose that we hadn't an ounce of silver or gold in the country and the government should issue two thousand millions of dollars in treasury notes receivable for taxes and a legal tender for all debts, public and private, do you imagine they would be worth anything—that they would command any of the products of labor? You know they would. And yet whatever worth or exchangeable value they had would be purely fiat, as I am not supposing that they are to be made redeemable in gold, silver, diamonds, or anything else under the sun. It is the demand for currency, primarily, which gives money its value, and not the material that composes it. When all the people realizes this fact we shall be nearing the day of financial emancipation.—(*Star Kansan*).

The people's party is the only party that proposes to issue a purely American money, based on American wealth for circulation among Americans, and from which neither American nor alien Shylocks can extort interest for its use by the American people. No more interest-bearing bonds for ever, is its motto.— (*Pittsburg Kansan*)

PREPARE FOR ACTION.

The Battle of Armagedden is at Hand—A Nation's Liberties at Stake.

The United States faces the greatest political contest of her history. The days of sham political battles are at an end on this coast. The mock wrath displayed by old party leaders in the presence of the rank and file, while behind the scenes they hob-nobbed with their political opponents, and proportioned the spoils, will be changed this year to a fight in earnest. The advent of populism, vigorous and confident, will force the use of tactics with which old partyites are ill-acquainted. Spread-eagle oratory and appeals to passion and prejudice, and bigotry don't go this year. Drafts drawn on long-gone records will be at a big discount in the coming campaign. ''What has your party been doing in the years since it made the records of which you boast?'' will be the question asked on every hand. The people have stopped banking on the deeds of their grand-fathers.'' ''What of the present?'' is the potent inquiry to-day. Stop shouting cant phrases and give us a reason for the faith within you, will be the demand on every fellow who bobs up to demand the suffrages of the people.

Poverty and bankruptcy, idleness and distress, crippled business and crushed industry, are as widespread as the boundaries of the nation. Concentration of wealth is the parent of it all. Special privilege was the instrumentality employed. All special privileges are legalized. The work that accomplished it covers a period of over thirty years. The record shows that both old parties were united in that work. The man who defends the record of either old party this year will be at a disadvantage. He will be simply defending a party whose votes in Congress helped to legalize every special privilege that has given to the idle schemers the power to absorb to themselves the product of the workers. Parties whose past has been a constant betrayal cannot be trusted for the future. The promises of parties that defend a record of betrayal and mismanagement are worthless.

The people will be told by old party men that the evils complained of by the populists were not caused by legislation and are beyond its reach. In the next breath they'll shout; ''Vote us and everything will be all right.'' Both these statements cannot be true. We have never had these evils only when legislation has robbed the masses of their natural rights and conferred special privileges on the classes. The development of hard times and the development of old party legislation have kept even pace with each other in this country.

Side by side along the same road have trotted the democratic and republican parties. Occasionally they have halted to engage in make-believe fight over some minor issue to hoodwink and deceive the rank and file. But all the time they have had an eye single to the one purpose of legislating in the interest of wealth and power. The motto has been: "To him that hath shall be given and from him who hath not shall be taken away even that which he hath."

Populism is a protest against special privilege. It is an organized effort of the people to regain their own. It is a battle for the producer and against the sponge. Its central idea is best expressed in the phrases: "He who will not work shall not eat," and he who cannot work shall not starve. The game of grab is played out when populism wins. Let every one who believes in justice and equality before the law, fall into line, under the banner of the new crusade, and never cease his efforts until the cause of humanity triumphs. Victory is in the air. Let every man do his duty.—(*Santa Cruz (Cal.) New Charter*).

CLEVERLY CAUGHT.

IT IS THE FIAT OF LAW WHICH GIVES TO METAL ITS MONETARY VALUE.

One of the country's milk and water bimetallist dailies declares that if Great Britain could be induced to adopt the double standard there would be no trouble in maintaining silver at par on the present ratio of 16 to 1. How so? We thought that silver was a naturally depreciated metal; that the silver dollar was worth only about 55 cents and that there was no power on earth that under present conditions could make it more valuable. It is a fact after all that the stamps of governments, the fiat of government, can make a dollar a dollar, regardless of its intrinsic value? It is true that if all governments should adopt the double standard it would cause an increased demand for silver, and its value would be correspondingly enhanced. If the government were willing to pay, or admitting silver to free coinage practically pay 100 cents for the amount of silver now in a silver dollar, it could not be bought for less. But the opponents of silver—including the daily referred to, we presume—deny the truth of that statement. They say that silver is depreciated and cannot be made equal to gold in intrinsic value. But here comes this daily and asserts its belief that the stamps of the United States and of Great Britain upon it would keep it at par. It admits all that the "fiat" money people have ever claimed, and if government stamps can make a "55 cent" silver dollar pass for 100 cents, they can make anything pass for a dollar. There is no getting away from the conclusion. If the premises are right the deduction is.—(*Farmers' Voice*) Ohio.

THE EUROPEAN LEVEL.

AMERICAN LABOR MAY HAVE TO COME TO IT, BUT THERE WILL
BE TROUBLE FIRST.

We have now a record of another case of anarchy in Columbus.

H. R. Johnson is the Vice President and Manager of the Columbus & Hocking Coal & Iron Co., a syndicate owning or controlling about 6,000 acres of coal land in the Hocking Valley. At the conference which took place in Lyndon hall, Columbus, on Saturday, June 2, between the miners and operators, Mr. Johnson was present as one of the delegates and spokesmen for the operators. Mr. William H. Crawford, of New Straitsville, Perry county, O., was present as a delegate on behalf of the miners. In that conference Mr. Johnson made use of the following language and treat to Mr. Crawford:

" It is not so much a question of price that shall be paid here and there, but a question of bringing the American workman down to the European level."

Mr. Crawford replied : "The Ohio miners stand firmly for 70 cents."

"Crawford," said Johnson, "your men are making a mistake in taking this stand ; the business of this country and the wages of this country must come down to a lower plane of prices. There must be a leveling-up process between this country and Europe. If you take that stand we will simply close our mines, and hunger, starvation and suffering will educate the American workmen to it."

Did anything more brutal and anarchistic ever escape the lips of man? — (*Ohio Populist*).

EDITORIAL *Chicago Times*, June 23rd, 1894.

What is this strange revelation made by examination of the books of the Santa Fe Railroad? Seven million dollars paid to shippers in rebates in the last four years in direct violation of the plain provisions of the inter-state commerce law? Will any of the officials of the railroad be indicted for this colossal law-breaking conspiracy? Is the matter to be brought to the attention of the federal grand jury? Will that eminent counsel to corporations, the attorney-general of the United States, take action against the insolvent violators of the law ? The attorney for the Santa Fe took a prominent part in the proceedings against Debs and others for violation of the inter-state commerce law. Did he go into court with clean hands or had he guilty knowledge of the way in which corporation was violating the same act ? These are very pertinent questions just now.

LORD MACAULAY'S PROPHECY.

In a letter written to Henry S. Randall of New York more than thirty-seven years ago Lord Macaulay prophesied many gloomy things of the American republic when it should become more populous. He foresaw in the constitution itself the seal of national disease and death, and looked upon the attempt to establish upon permanent foundations a government of and by the people as utterly futile. In that letter Lord Macaulay said :

I have not the smallest doubt that, if we had a purely democratic government here, either the poor would plunder the rich and civilization would perish, or order and property would be saved by a strong military government, and liberty would perish. You may think that your country enjoys an exemption from these evils. I will frankly own to you that I am of a very different opinion. Your fate I believe to be certain, though it is deferred by a physical cause. As long as you have a boundless extent of fertile and unoccupied land your laboring population will be far more at ease than the laboring population of the old world ; and, while that is the case, the Jeffersonian policy may continue to exist without causing any fatal calamity. But the time will come when New England will be as thickly peopled as old England. Wages will be as low, and will fluctuate as much with you as with us. You will have your Manchesters and Birminghams ; and, in those Manchesters and Birminghams, hundreds of thousands of artizans will assuredly be sometimes out of work. * * * The day will come when, in the state of New York, a multitude of people, none of whom has had more than half a breakfast, or expects to have more than half a dinner, will choose a legislature. Is it possible to doubt what sort of legislature will be chosen ? There will be, I fear spoliation. The spoliation will increase the distress. The distress will produce fresh spoliation. There is nothing to stop you. Your constitution is all sail and no anchor. As I have said before, when a society has entered on this downward progress, either civilization or liberty must perish. Either some Cæsar or Napoleon will seize the reins of government with a strong hand, or your republic will be as fearfully plundered and laid waste by barbarians in the twentieth century as the Roman empire was in the fifth, with this difference, that the Huns and Vandals who ravaged the Roman Empire came from without, while your Huns and Vandals will have been engendered within your own country by your own institutions.

Lord Macaulay feared the spoliation of the rich by the poor. The history of this country for the last thirty years, on the contrary, is one disgraceful record of the spoliation of the poor by the combined forces of the corrupt and avaricious monopolized capital. The protest of the people, in which the plutocratic press professes to see the fulfillment of Macaulay's prophecy that it must encroach no further upon the people's rights. It is not directed against the rich ; it simply advises them that those who labor have rights which must not be trampled under foot. The people demand nothing from capital save that it keep hands off the inherent and inalien- able rights of all. The movement is not an assault ; it is a defence against the aggressions of combined political and commercial brigandage which would place the people under perpetual tribute to the few. It is an empathic reiteration of the just principle communicated by Thomas Jefferson, when Lord Macaulay, true to his lordly scorn of the plain people, so much despised : "Equal and exact justice to all, special privileges to none " Not much resemblance in that to the mob of the proletariat working destruction and desolation, which Macaulay's distorted vision foresaw. (*Chicago Times*).

ON THE BRINK OF BONDS.

GOLD RESERVE GRADUALLY DWINDLES BEFORE THE ASSAULTS OF CLEVELAND, WALL STREET & CO.

There is no cowardly equivocation or beating about the bush in the style in which the special correspondent of the great Jeffersonian democratic daily, the Chicago *Times*, dishes up the news from Washington, as follows :

The thermometer notifies one that this is no time to nurse excitement. Therefore let us be cool. The country is again on the brink of bonds. Possibly $70,000,000 this time. You have not heard of bonds for a week. That is because bonds were drawing near. Right now bonds are crouching in the underbrush of the coming week like a tiger about to spring. Curtis, Carlisle's understudy, came in from New York last night. He has as near as may be finished all bond arrangements. The last one heard of bonds was about six days ago. Car- lisle sprang into voluntary print via the press associations with the word that no more bonds would be issued. As they say in the whale-killing business, it was simply a case with Carlisle of "up flukes." Our treasurer merely dived. The whale "sounded." The next time—and almost of a verity within ten days—you see Carlisle in this affair. He will come to the surface and spout bonds. To-day the gold reserve went below $70,000,000, As our valuable treasury closed its game for the day the figures, in truth, were lower than $69,000,000. That is the figure to which the conspirators, whose firm epithet is Cleveland, Wall Street & Co,, have been scheming to descend. And now come bonds.

It is a plot, a plain plot, without frills or fixings. During the last month.

May, our famous treasurer sold or paid out $32,000,000 of gold. This makes the record. It is a million more of gold than was ever paid out in one month by our treasury in the long history of the government. During our whole civil war no such bleeding of gold occurred. Thirty-one millions in one month was the worst which ever chanced before. This May-day gold outburst—thirty-two unexpected, record-breaking millions—smells mightily like a vast rat. Another remarkable feature, aside from the utter silence which has waited on the transaction, is that Carlisle's books depict the fact that every dollar of his vast out-go went to redeem greenbacks. Cleveland, Wall Street & Co. mean to keep within the law while founding the second bond edifice, and quiet word went about to the conspirators on the outside to present nothing but greenbacks for gold. Friction must be avoided and no basis for carping criticism must exist that gold had been paid out for silver notes and similar chips and whetstones which legally do not demand gold.

"Bring nothing but greenbacks when you come for gold, and make no noise," was the message, shod with wool, which was sent the noiseless rounds by Cleveland, Wall Street & Co., to the firm's bond pals on the outside. Of course Carlisle cut the greenbacks thus received immediately loose again in the forty avenues through which your Uncle Sam spends money, so they could be at once re-collected by the bond sharps and sent up again wherewith to buy more gold. Well, that's all there is to it. The barometer is falling and it's going to presently storm bonds.

By the way, in the Chicago *Times* the people's cause has a powerful advocate and, although nominally a democratic paper, the *Times* fills a want long felt by the populists of the territory tributary and contiguous to Chicago. It matters not by what name a paper chooses to be called, so long as it battles for the principles of justice, equity and righteousness and stands for the cause of pure democracy and against the rule of encroaching monopoly and a plutocratic oligarchy. This the Chicago *Times* does, and its editorial columns are daily replete with advanced ideas in line with organized labor demands. Then, the *Times* has opened a department which it calls the "People's Forum," to which it admits communications discussing the live issues of the day and reform ideas in general. Let every reformer drop a card to the *Times* bidding it Godspeed. EDITORIAL *Cincinnatian*, June 30, 1894.

EDITORIAL *Cincinnati Enquirer*, Sept. 25, 1894.

A PLEA FOR SELF-GOVERNMENT.

Is it not about time for the people of the United States to govern themselves by insuring the enforcement of laws enacted by their representatives in Congress? This they can only do through the executive branch of the Government, and when that fails, the republic is being for the time subverted. The people in this country are the supreme power. They made the constitution, and they have amended it. It is the ultimate expression of their will as to the distribution of their powers. The statutes enacted by Congress under that constitution are the supreme law of the land. The President has no more right to disobey one of these laws than has the humblest citizen. He cannot enter upon the duties of his office until he takes a solemn oath to see that all the laws are executed faithfully. For him to set up his judgment against any law of the land, and to neglect its enforcement because he thinks it unwise, is not only an impertinence, but a high crime, for which the constitution provides that he may be impeached and removed from office, and made forever ineligible to hold office under the Government of the United States. Every man is free to express his opinion as to the wisdom or folly of any statute, and to advocate its amendment or appeal, but he has no right to obstruct its execution while it continues to be law.

We are led to these observations by the flippancy with which a numerous faction in this country, including the President and his Cabinet in its numbers, repudiates and obstructs the execution of the laws concerning money. The law which makes the standard silver dollar a legal tender, equally with the standard gold dollar, has been treated with derision and contempt during the past sixteen years by Presidents and Secretaries of the Treasury. That dollar has been denounced as a "clipped" dollar, a "dishonest" dollar and a "fifty cents" dollar. Upon every silver certificate issued under the Bland-Allison act of 1878 is printed a declaration that the silver dollar it represents is in the Treasury and belongs to the holder of that certificate, and also that the certificate is receivable for all dues to the Government. These certificates were issued for the convenience of the public, " *because any man would rather carry a paper note in his pocket than either a gold or a silver coin.*" Among the devices resorted to by the Treasury department to make the silver dollar unpopular has been that of paying out inconvenient amounts of silver instead of silver certificates. Government employees have been made to receive silver dollars instead of silver certificates in the hope that the increase in the actual silver circulation would make silver unpopular. Among the falsehoods circulated industriously by the gold advocates, in and out of office, is that which asserts that it is impossible to keep silver money in circulation. The falsehood in this consists in withholding the fact that, for the silver dollars in the Treasury, paper certificates to the full extent of them are in circulation. Secretaries of the Treasury have insulted the intelligence of the people by complaining that the coining of dollars would have to be stopped because the vaults of the Treasury were crowded. Every man of any sense knows that it would cost but little time or money to build vaults that would contain all the silver in the world. If there is a surplus wheat crop, new warehouses are built, and, in view of the unoccupied space in the United States, it would not seem difficult to provide room for an additional few feet of storage room if the same should be needed for silver dollars, represented by silver certificates in circulation among the people.

But Government officials have not contented themselves with deriding the law which makes the silver dollar a legal tender. They have refused to execute it. They have refused to treat it as the money of redemption, which it is under the plain letter of the law. They have clamorously asserted that, despite the law, the Treasury Department would redeem its notes only in gold. This was accompanied with declarations to the effect that the standard silver dollar coined under the law, and its value fixed by the law was not of that value. The constitution provides that Congress shall have the power "to coin money and regulate the value thereof," Presidents and Secretaries of the Treasury and their . underlings, strikers and spokesmen, have filled the air with their noisy din that Congress should not fix the value of the money coined under its laws. The constitution never provided that the coin value of money should be regulated by a manufactured market price for bullion. It did not provide that an artificial price for silver bullion should be created by shutting the doors of the mints against it, and that from that time forward silver dollars should be worth only what they would fetch by the pound after being melted up. It provided that the value fixed by Congress should be the value of all coins, and, thus far, the opponents of silver have not been able to reduce the value of the silver dollar the least fraction of a cent below the value of a gold dollar. Where can you buy in this country more goods for one hundred gold dollars than for one hundred silver dollars?

The resumption act of 1875 took effect in 1879, when John Sherman was Secretary of the Treasury. Although the Bland-Allison act of the previous year had restored, with its full legal tender quality, the silver dollar, which Mr. Sherman had surreptitiously abolished in 1873, he commenced the policy of treating gold coins as the only money of redemption. He piled up $100,000,000 of gold in the Treasury with which to redeem the greenbacks. *Nobody wanted the silver or gold either*, and so the people kept their greenbacks, and the Treasury kept its gold. But in all the public utterances of Mr. Sherman and his successors, and of the Presidents who appointed them, the world had been given to understand that the laws of Congress concerning silver money were not to be treated as laws by the Executive branch of the Government, but only as the vaporings of lunatics.

Under the Bland-Allison act only two million dollars a month of silver were being coined. The people chafed at this restriction and at their congressional elections sent free coinage majorities to Congress and re-enforced the silver majorities in the Senate. Then was playing upon the people the monumental fraud of the Sherman purchase act. Under this purchase and coinage of two millions of dollars of silver per month was stopped, and the purchase of four millions of ounces per month was substituted. For this Treasury notes were to be issued, and the silver bullion so purchased was by the law required to be coined as rapidly as the Secretary of the Treasury deemed necessary for the redemption of the Treasury notes with which it was purchased. These notes were made payable in "coin," and so read upon their face. Then, as if to remove all doubt that coin included silver as well as gold, the law provided in express words that the notes should be payable in either silver or gold, at the option of the Secretary of the Treasury. This guarantee of the use of silver dollars in the redemption of the Treasury notes has been made a nullity by the Treasury Department, commencing when Charles Foster was Secretary of the Treasury. He decided in the interest of the Austrian Government, which then needed our gold, that he would exercise his option under the Sherman act by redeeming in gold only the notes issued only for the purchase of silver bullion. Having thus decided that he would not pay out any silver coin for the redemption of these notes, it naturally followed that the amount of silver bullion necessary to be coined for their redemption would be simply none at all. This encouraged the foreign bankers to drain our Treasury of gold, which they did by buying silver bullion and exchange it with the Government for Treasury notes, and then demanding the gold coin for those notes. Thus we exchanged our gold for their silver and allowed the silver thus bought to accumulate instead of being coined. Then came the outcry that we were buying "pig metal," which would have to be sold by the pound. The purchase of it was stopped by the repeal of the Sherman purchasing act, but the promise to provide for coining all silver as well as all gold which might be presented at our mints, without any discrimination against either, has not only never been performed, but it has been treated by the gold faction as a monstrous proposition recently heard of for the first time.

These perversions of the law by the Treasury Department are violations of the law. The attempt to discredit any coin of the United States is an obstruction to the execution of the coinage laws.

The foregoing review of the silver situation seems called for at this time by the renewed activity by the gold speculators, and their instruments in office, in their opposition to free silver coinage. They have been suddenly aroused by the trumpet call of the Ohio Democracy for the restoration of silver to the side of its companion, gold, as the money of the constitution. They appear to believe that the people rule in this country only by their consent, and their representative have no right to frame laws, and have them executed, which are not approved by dealers in gold. But the people are likely to move on without regard to their frantic outcries, and in 1896 they will not make the mistake which they made in 1892—of electing a Congress largely in favor of free silver and a President bound hand and foot to the service of the gold kings. They will choose a Chief Magistrate who will execute the laws concerning money which their representative will enact. We hail the violence of the gold press as proof that they read the handwriting on the wall, and that the deliverance of the Ohio Democratic State Convention on the subject of silver is properly regarded by them as the most important step yet taken in the campaign for the redress of wrongs long endured. Free silver will be the banner cry of the Democracy in 1896, and there acts will be recruited by the advocates of free coinage throughout the land without regard to previous party affiliations.

JOHN SHERMAN AND AN HONEST DOLLAR.

Senator Sherman is reported as renewing his devotion to what he calls the "honest dollar." Mr. Sherman's idea of an honest dollar is one that is made heavier from time to time, so that it will buy more goods and pay more debts than before. More than any other man in the whole world he is responsible for the demonetization of silver throughout the world. The European mints were not closed to silver until Mr. Sherman had guaranteed that the United States would pursue a similar policy. Having sold us all out to the great bond brokers of London and Germany, he delivered the goods by stealth. Uncle Sam was blindfolded by him and led into the pit of the gold standard of 1873. He had struggled ever since to get out of that pit, and, in 1878, and again in 1890, was about to stand once more on firm ground, when political jugglers, engineered by John Sherman, tripped him, and, by their dexterity, overcame his giant strength and sent him again into the pit.

By the demonetization of silver Mr. Sherman inaugurated the era of dishonest money. By an act of legislative trickery he increased the value of every dollar in the United States by two-thirds. He did not do this by adding to the weight of each dollar, but he reduced the number of dollars. What would the world have said, and what would the American people have said, if they had discovered that Mr. Sherman had changed our dollar in such a way as to put two dollars into one—one being gold and the other silver? Did he not do exactly the equivalent of this when he drove out the silver dollar, and left only the gold dollar to stand for both? Dollars are valuable in proportion to the number of them in existence. The gold men all tell us this whenever there is any movement to increase the volume of money. They are then greatly alarmed about the disasters that will follow inflation. They deprecate any increase in the number of dollars, because, they say, the price of commodoties will increase, and that this will lead to wild speculation. It is perfectly clear that if an increase of the number of dollars in the world will injure the owner of money, by diminishing the purchasing power of each dollar, then any reduction in the number of dollars in the world must injure the owners of any other kinds of property by increasing the purchasing power of each dollar and reducing the number of dollars for which any given commodity will sell. Any interference with the number of dollars in the world, except by such an increase of them as is rendered necessary by the steady increase of the business use for money, is a crime of the same nature that an alteration in the length of a yard stick, the size of a bushel measure, or of any means of ascertaining quantities would be. When Mr. Sherman abolished the silver dollar he added to the mortgage on every man's farm and every mechanic's home an additional burden, making him owe one hundred and sixty-seven dollars for every one hundred dollars that he owed before that time. Contraction does the same injury to the debtor class that inflation does to the creditor class.

The world's business is largely transacted upon faith. The sovereign power to coin money and to regulate its value is laid by every nation, to be exercised for the protection of the people, and to hold the balance equal between those who borrow and those who lend. When a Government allows itself to become an instrument of oppression and to alter the relation between money and other property, it commits an act of confiscation. It does worse than that, it creates the apprehension that the same thing will be repeated whenever the interest, or rather the avarice of usurers, may demand it. Mr. Sherman has led his Government into the commission of this crime. He has abolished honest money in this country by lessening the number of dollars, and thereby increasing the value of each dollar. Those who seek to repair this wrong and to restore silver to the place it occupied in our money system prior to 1873 are the only advocates of honest money.

The advocates of dishonest money, although a pitiful minority, hope to prevent the restoration of silver coinage in the future as they have in the past, by the corrupt use of money. They do not have to control many men. If they can name the Speaker of the House of Representatives he can easily prevent the consideration of a free coinage bill. If they have a majority of one in the

Finance Committee of the Senate they can stifle a free coinage bill in committee. But if, unfortunately for them, a vote is forced in both Houses and a free coinage bill is passed, they must then have a President who will veto the bill. The Bland-Allison Act, which permitted the purchase and coinage of two millions of silver dollars per month, was passed over the veto of President Hayes in 1878. The gold ring, taking warning from that, has never permitted a free coinage bill to reach the President. Several times they have succeeded in choking such a measure to death in the meshes of parliamentary rules in the House. During Mr. Cleveland's first term and during Mr. Harrison's term the restoration of free coinage was only prevented by preventing a vote from being taken in the House of Representatives.

Thus dishonest money has been perpetuated in this country by the same power that inaugurated it. If Mr. Sherman really wants to see an honest dollar made current in this country, let him leave the service of the gold ring, and aid in undoing the wrong which he engineered in 1873. Let him aid in preventing the emissaries of foreign bankers and their American correspondents from corrupting our State and National Conventions. Let him join the friends of honest money in selecting for his party a Presidential candidate who will honestly serve the people, instead of dishonestly serving the money power, who will not barter the official appointments within his gift for votes against the free coinage of silver ; who will not dishearten the advocates of silver by threatening to crush with his veto any silver measure that may be laid before him, but who will, on the contrary sympathize with the people in their desire to remove the yoke of their present taskmasters, and to restore the measure of values which includes silver with gold as the basis of our money system.

Mr. Sherman is an old man. It has been in his power to do more harm to his countrymen than they have suffered from all other causes during the nation's existence, and he has fully improved his opportunity. The industries of this country have for many years been afflicted with a creeping paralysis by his course on the silver question. They exhibit no signs of improvement. The reduction of duties on imports does not seem to have revived importations. The greatest boon which could come, and one that would revive the spirits of our people and lead to legislation that would restore prosperity, would be the conversion of John Sherman from his present ways. If he could be made to see a great light, like that which blinded Saul on his way to Damascus, and if, like Saul, he could be changed from doing evil to doing good, he would be looked upon for all time to come as the benefactor of his race. He would then see in circulation the honest dollar for which he says he is longing—a dollar that would only buy a dollar's worth, a dollar that would extinguish a dollar of indebtedness ; a dollar that would bring the farmer's products to their former standard ; a dollar which would, by its stability in value, encourage enterprises and remove the congestion of money in the great banking centers, caused by the fear of investing in the face of continually falling prices ; a dollar that would take the place of the dishonest dollar created under the leadership of Mr. Sherman to enable money lenders to convert other people's property to their own uses without consideration.

The Democratic party of Ohio waits for no man's conversion. With a deep sense of its responsibility for having allowed Mr. Sherman to represent Ohio in the Senate, it leads the way in the restoration of silver coinage, which he abolished. It exhorts all who believe in honest money to join in this year in placing Ohio on the right side of the question.

EDITORIAL *Cincinnati Enquirer*, Oct. 30th 1894.

WHY AMERICA IS INCREASING IN CRIME?

I've been thinking, Uncle Sam, I've been thinking,
  And my thoughts I can scarcely define ;
I've been thinking why people can wonder
  At America's increase of crime.
Cries old Uncle Sam : It's a poser,
  There is something I can't understand ;
I would give up a trifle to know, sir,
  Why crime should increase in our land—
We have plenty of gold, I am told, sir ;
We have heaps laid away in the store, sir,
Guarded with bolts and bars, sir,
  And still there is an increase of crime.

Stop Uncle Sam, please stop,
  And if you do you will be on top.
Change your mind, don't issue bond,
  Because that is what the Banker's want.
You want to know the reason why !   ·
  Your pile goes low and their's goes high.

It's quite true what you say, Uncle Samuel,
  We have gold laid away in store,
Mouldy with mildew and rust, sir,
  And guarded with heavy iron doors ;
While you, like a dog in your manger,
  Your gold to yourself you confine,
When a little would make a great change, sir,
  In this terrible increase of crime--
For expense you don't care a jot, sir ;
Politicians you feed a whole lot, sir,
While the poor man with hunger may rot, sir.
  And still there is an increase of crime.

Stop, Uncle Sam, please stop,
  And if you do you will be on top.
Change your mind, don't issue bond,
  Because that is what the Banker's want.
You want to know the reason why !
  Your pile goes low and their's goes high.

Can you wonder at crime—can you wonder,
  When you meet the police, on their beat,
Arresting the poor car-monger
  For earning his bread in the street ?
While the thief on the corner stands grinning
  In the broad open light of the day ;
Your pockets he will pick for a shilling,
  And the law cannot touch him, they say—
While he laughs with contempt and derision,
Defies all your police division,
This poor carter you cast into prison,
  Uncle Sam, can you wonder at crime ?

Stop Uncle Sam, please stop,
  And if you do you will be on top.
Change your mind, don't issue bond,
  Because that is what the Banker's want.
You want to know the reason why !
  Your pile goes low and their's goes high.

It's quite true what you say, Uncle Sam, sir,
  Temptation is hard to resist,
Just look at our poor needle girls, sir,
  Trying their best to subsist ,
Can you wonder at their prostitution,
  When blood-sucking firms barely give
Enough to ward off destitution ?
  Although she is poor, she must live—
There is our poor servant girl, God defend her,
  With feelings as pure and tender
As our proud city ladies, remember—
  Uncle Sam, can you wonder at crime ?

Stop Uncle Sam, please stop,
  And if you do you will be on top.
Change your mind, don't issue bond,
  Because that is what the Banker's want.
You want to know the reason why !
  Your pile goes low and their's goes high.

Just think while you are drinking your wine, sir,
  How the poor of our land they are fed,
While you with your rich folks can dine, sir,
  'Tis a God-send for them to get bread ;
Go visit the house of the poor, sir,
  Such sights you will never behold—
The prison dens go and expose, sir,
  Then scatter your hoarding of gold—
When a little would soon break asunder
  The chains that the poor sufferer is under,
Go list to that great voice of hunger,
  And never more wonder at crime.

Stop Uncle Sam, please stop,
  And if you do you will be on top.
Change your mind, don't issue bond,
  Because that is what the Banker's want.
You want to know the reason why !
  Your pile goes low and their's goes high !

Ambition sure with patience bore,
  Money-changers' Trust are in vain ;
McKinley-Hanna better have stayed home
  And eased their foolish pain.
Stop their object for they are for gain,
Cease their hope for the ambition is vain.
Calm the tumult of your breast,
For bi-metallist will vote you to rest.

McKinley-Hanna will have a better opinion of the people after election.

In concluding, I quote an extract from an English financial newspaper published after the defeat of the Dingley Bill:

MARCH 10, 1896.—The *London Financial News* says:

The *financial situation* in the United States is *very serious*. The Senate has blocked all relief measures proposed by President Cleveland, and Congress is at a dead standstill on the money question. The Free Coinage Senators are masters of the situation. The condition of affairs in the United States demands the *immediate attention of British financiers and statesmen*. The *trade* of the *world* is in *our hands*, but it will *not long remain there* if the United States goes to a bimetallic basis, with free and unlimited coinage of silver. With the addition of silver to the volume of money, *everything in America* would take on a new face ; labor and all industry would gain *new life*. The *grip* of the *Gold Standard* on the products of the world would be loosened and *prices would rise*. Great Britain would *lose her markets* in South America, Asia and Europe, and American ships would not be long in capturing the carrying trade of the world. British creditors must now apply themselves quickly to the American money problem.

The sound money men and Banking interests, led by *Senator Sherman, Cleveland* and *Carlisle*, with *plentiful supply of means*, have been beaten. The American people are now thoroughly aroused and educated on the power and *use of money*, and *made desperate by debt and business depression* they are forcing *free silver* as the main issue. Great Britain need fear no injury to her trade or investments if the *Republican party* can force "protective tariff" as the main issue in the coming Presidential campaign. But if free silver dominates the American minds and carries it to the polls, it will bring about a change in England that will be *ruinous* from its suddenness and severity. The damage that can be done British manufactures by a *protective tariff is slight* compared with the *disasters* that would be entailed by a *change* from a *single gold* to a complete bimetallic standard. It is evident that the Democratic party will not renominate a man who holds President Cleveland's ideas on money, and the only hope for a *continuation of Mr. Cleveland's financial policy* will be in the success of the Republicans in the next election. The success of free coinage will bring down the rate of interest on money and cause an immediate rise in the price of all commodities. When silver becomes primary money the American mines will pour their products into the mints, and a *new era*, similar to that produced by the *issue of greenbacks* during the Civil War will begin. Gold will leave the banks and enter into competition with silver in the avenues of trade, and the manufactories of the United States, which have been shut down or *crippled* since 1892, will *again resume their fight* for English markets. It is doubtful whether the Republican party can be held much longer in check by sound money statesmen, as its adherents are divided by powerful factions. The Democratic party is also breaking up under the weight of the free silver agitation. It matters not to Great Britain which party succeeds if the *gold standard is maintained*, but if either of the old parties or a new party goes into power pledged to *free coinage*, it will be inimical and prejudicial to *English manufactories and trade*.

The American people cling with wonderful tenacity to party organization, but *financial embarassment and business stagnation* has become *too severe* for their patience, and they are ready for *any change that promises relief*. They are becoming convinced that it cannot be found in the protection theory, as that has been *tried*, and they are massing now on *free silver*. When that issue comes *fairly* before the *American people* England will regret her apathy and adherence to the gold standard.

.